More than
PETTICOATS

Remarkable
Nevada
Women

April '06

Cyndy —

Enjoy the remarkable
women of Nevada.

Jan Cleere

MORE THAN PETTICOATS SERIES

MORE THAN PETTICOATS

REMARKABLE NEVADA WOMEN

Jan Cleere

TWODOT®

GUILFORD, CONNECTICUT
HELENA, MONTANA

AN IMPRINT OF THE GLOBE PEQUOT PRESS

A · T W O D O T® · B O O K

Copyright © 2005 by The Globe Pequot Press

TwoDot is a registered trademark of The Globe Pequot Press.

Cover photo: Two teachers in cowgirl hats. Courtesy of Nevada Historical Society

Library of Congress Cataloging-in-Publication Data is available.

ISBN 0-7627-2739-X

Manufactured in the United States of America
First Edition/First Printing

To my daughter Kathy, a remarkable woman in any state.

CONTENTS

$\mathscr{A}$CKNOWLEDGMENTS

$\mathscr{T}$he following individuals and organizations provided me with assistance. Without their generosity, my task would have been just that—a task—and not the wonderful adventure I experienced as I delved into Nevada's golden history.

My sincerest thanks to Carrie Townley Porter, president of the Nevada Women's History Project, whose support and wealth of knowledge made my journey so delightful.

Special thanks to Shirlaine Baldwin for sharing the story of her grandmother, Ah Cum Kee.

Former Daughter of Charity Georgia Hedrick provided insight into the everyday lives of the Daughters, as did Carolyn Beaupre and Sister Margaret Ann Gainey.

Cherry Jones willingly offered her knowledge of Eliza Cook and introduced me to Eliza's great-niece Janice Hansen, who related family stories about her Auntie Cook.

Tamera Buzick led me around the grounds of Washoe Valley's Bowers Mansion in the middle of a snowstorm, answering my unending questions about Alison Bowers.

The staff of the Nevada Historical Society, Reno, particularly librarian Michael Maher, helped me locate elusive articles and photographs. I am also grateful to the librarians at the Las Vegas Branch of the society for their assistance.

In Reno, Robert E. Blesse, head of the University of Nevada Special Collections, and Kathryn Totton, photograph and map curator, were generous with their support, as was librarian Jonnie Kennedy at the university's Las Vegas Special Collections.

At the Nevada State Library & Archives in Carson City, Joyce Cox, head of library services, provided numerous documents,

Acknowledgments

books, and videos. The administrative assistant for archives and records, Guy Rocha, graciously e-mailed me answers to my last-minute questions.

I would also like to thank Wynne Brown, Sue Fawn Chung, Joanne Goodwin, and Sally Zanjani for the parts they played in assisting me with this project.

The collections at the Arizona Historical Society and the University of Arizona libraries contain innumerable and invaluable books and articles on Nevada history. Thank you, Arizona, for being so interested in your sister state.

And to my family who endured a year of empty pantry shelves and cold suppers as my eyes never left the computer screen, thank you for your love and encouragement.

INTRODUCTION

When reporter Mark Twain entered the desert town of Carson, Nevada, in the mid-1800s, he described his destination as "a desert, walled in by barren, snow-clad mountains. There was not a tree in sight. There was no vegetation but the endless sagebrush and greasewood. All nature was gray with it. We were plowing through great depths of powdery alkali dust that rose in thick clouds and floated across the plain like smoke from a burning house. . . . we and the sagebrush and the other scenery were all one monotonous color."

Several years later the author Idah Meacham Strobridge viewed the Nevada terrain as resplendent with "golden sunlight and purple shadows." "If you love the Desert, and live in it, and lie awake at night under its low-hanging stars, you know you are a part of the pulse-beat of the universe, and you feel the swing of the spheres through space. And you hear through the silence the voice of God speaking."

How differently we view our surroundings. One individual sees a bleak and desolate wasteland, while another describes her home as resplendent in color, an almost religious experience. The women who first trekked across Nevada Territory's rough terrain most certainly envisioned the land from diverse viewpoints. But something held them there. Few of the women in this book left Nevada once they smelled the sweet mountain air or tasted the gritty sand between their teeth.

Miners Ferminia Sarras and Josie Pearl made and lost fortunes through their years roaming Nevada's hills, but neither sought to leave her rocky confines for more luxurious surroundings.

Educator Maude Frazier found her treks along Nevada's dusty trails exhilarating as she watched ". . . the ever-changing lights and shadows on the far mountains, the gorgeous desert flora. . . ." Attorney Felice Cohn and physician Eliza Cook found more than enough to keep them tied to the state as they strived to improve the lives of women and children who sought freedom from illness, poverty, intolerance, even violence. After the death of her husband, Helen Stewart continued to work their southern Nevada ranch, and then witnessed the first glimmer of neon lights along Las Vegas's then desolate streets.

Of the women who left Nevada, none succeeded in brushing the dust from her clothes or the beauty of the land from her thoughts. Idah Strobridge wrote pages describing the "mauve-tinged mountains" she left behind. From her California home, suffragist and politician Anne Henrietta Martin implored Nevada officials to entice and promote new businesses if they wanted the state to lose its "ugly duckling" reputation. Alison Bowers lost her family and fortune in the golden hills of Nevada, but she would not leave the meadows of Washoe Valley until forced to do so.

Some women were bound to the land. Sarah Winnemucca Hopkins fought to keep her Paiute people within the territory of their ancestors, while an uneducated Washoe woman, Dat so la lee, wove her way into the hearts of Nevadans with the intricacy of her baskets designed from native materials. Despite the odds against her, Ah Cum Kee found stability in the state's less-than-fertile soil, establishing herself as Nevada's first Chinese woman farmer.

Nevadans sometimes had to look long and hard to find beauty along the rowdy streets of early mining towns such as Virginia City. When the Daughters of Charity arrived on the Comstock, they gathered up the orphaned and abandoned children, even the "soiled doves," tucking all under the protective wings of their wide cornettes.

All these women saw what could be, not what was, and they determined that this barren land was habitable and lovely and grand, making it the ideal spot to settle down, produce children, and raise havoc when education and social progress needed a determined yet compassionate hand.

The photo on the front cover of this book depicts two sisters, Pearl and Carol Ivins. The Ivins sisters, five in all, taught in seven different one-room schoolhouses around Nevada during the early 1900s. Nevada's future lay in their hands, as it did with every teacher who ventured down a dirt-encrusted trail, swept the dust from her desk, and opened up children's minds.

Today the legacy of teachers such as the Ivins sisters, as well as all Nevada's pioneering women, continues through the work of the Nevada Women's History Project (NWHP). Started in 1994, the statewide organization serves as an educational, nonprofit venture "providing visibility and support for the gathering and dissemination of history about the roles and contributions of Nevada women of every race, class, and ethnic background." The NWHP presents programs and projects across the state promoting the women who endured the harshness of the Nevada terrain in order to build a home, rear a family, and pave the way toward stability and equality.

After I saw Nevada's mauve-tinged mountains and purple shadows that Idah Strobridge wrote about so many years ago, I understood why pioneering women fell in love with this country and stayed. The Sagebrush State, or Silver State—both nomenclatures aptly describe Nevada—boasts 110,000 square miles of piñon and ancient bristlecone pine trees, sagebrush flowers tempting the appetites of slow-moving desert tortoises, desert bighorn sheep crowned with massive curled horns, and mountain bluebirds singing from the highest snowcapped mountaintops. With gold and silver dominating the myriad ores located across the state, Nevada attracts the bold and brave, the daring and daredevil.

There are many other remarkable Nevada women, like the Ivins sisters, whose stories are not told between the pages of this book. I urge you to seek them out, discover their uniqueness, and pass along their histories to your children and grandchildren. Only then will their lives be truly complete.

ALISON ORAM BOWERS

1826–1903

Eilley's Millions

Welcome to Bowers Mansion! Alison Bowers could have shouted the words from the rooftop of her new home in Nevada Territory's Washoe Valley, thousands of miles from her native Scotland. She lovingly admired the furnishings she and her husband, Sandy, had purchased on a grand European adventure: fireplace mantels sculpted from Italian marble, elaborate furniture, paintings by renowned artists. More than 1,000 leather-bound books lined her library shelves waiting to be read. She gently fingered the silver table service designed by a French silversmith. Gold and silver doorknobs adorned every room of the mansion. Her wine cellar held vintages from the finest vineyards in France. And just outside her front door, she had lined her veranda with ivy brought all the way from England's Westminster Abbey, mingling it with Scottish broom gathered in her homeland.

Although short and stout, Alison—or Eilley, as she was better known—almost floated across the specially designed carpets as she traipsed from room to room. Her blue glacé silk dress, an original Paris design, was adorned with sprigs of apple blossom gar-

Alison Bowers

lands and ribbons that fluttered in the glow of hundreds of candles as if tiny fireflies had invaded her luxurious home. All her efforts, and so much money, had brought to fruition her childhood vision of living in a mansion set against a backdrop of majestic mountains and lush meadows.

As a young girl growing up in Scotland, usually standing over a steaming pot of stew or mound of dirty clothing, young Eilley Oram (sometimes spelled *Orrum*) often envisioned a life surrounded by snowcapped mountains from which trickling streams meandered into meadows resplendent with flowers. Many Scottish women were said to be clairvoyant, so it was not unusual that she had these vivid dreams. Eilley also treasured her "peep stone," an oval glass ball that Scottish seeresses claimed gave them insight into future events.

Born in the Royal Burgh of Forfar, Scotland, on September 6, 1826, one of ten children, Eilley wanted more than the poor farmland her father toiled, more than the backbreaking housework her mother endured. When the opportunity arose to flee the cold muddy shores of her heritage, she left with little regret.

Members of the Church of Jesus Christ of Latter Day Saints recruited widely across Europe, seeking members to join their new colony in America. Eilley felt no particular affiliation to Mormon beliefs but accepted the faith to escape the drudgery that awaited her if she stayed in Scotland. At the age of fifteen, and with the disapproval of her parents, she left for America.

Accompanied by her married sister Betsy, and Betsy's husband, Eilley arrived in Nauvoo, Illinois, in 1841. The following year she married a fellow Scotsman, the widower Stephen Hunter, who was thirty years her senior. The couple soon joined the exodus of Mormons heading for Utah Territory's Great Salt Lake Valley.

Throughout her marriage to Hunter, Eilley watched fervently

for signs she was pregnant. When no children were forthcoming, Hunter looked about for another wife to give him heirs. Polygamy was legal within the Mormon community, but Eilley had no desire to share her husband with another woman. She paid $15 to divorce Hunter in 1850, then supported herself by working in a Salt Lake general store.

She married again in 1853. Alexander Cowan, a hardworking farmer, had no desire to take more than one wife. In fact, he was hard pressed to afford even one.

When Mormon leader Brigham Young called for the establishment of new colonies in uncharted western lands, the Cowans sold their meager farm and in 1855 ventured to the new settlement of Mormon Station, near present-day Carson City. They soon moved on to Washoe Valley and the newly established community of Franktown. These Mormon settlements would eventually become part of Nevada Territory.

Arriving in Washoe Valley, Eilley saw the snow atop towering Mount Rose. She watched the streams flowing into the lush valley below. When she put her hand into a spring and discovered hot water bubbling forth, she told her husband to purchase the land— this was where they would settle. For about $100, the Cowans bought 320 acres that already included a roughly hewn log house.

The spring and summer months brought bountiful crops. But when winter set in, the ground froze and little could be accomplished until it thawed. Eilley convinced Cowan to build a boardinghouse across the hill in an area miners wistfully called Gold Canyon. Stragglers from spent California gold mines had heard rumors of promising ore veins in these Nevada hills since 1850, but so far little had been found to warrant much interest.

In her Scottish brogue, Eilley called her mule trips from Washoe Valley to Gold Canyon "goin' over the hell." She fed her boarders and cleaned their clothes, bringing in enough money to sustain the Cowans through the hard, cold winter months.

A handful of miners worked Nevada's barren hills. In their zeal for gold, they threw away the black, gooey sand that covered their meager strikes, believing it nothing but filthy sludge. This silt, however, contained valuable deposits of silver that would soon create the impetus for thousands to leave their homes and head for Nevada.

In 1857 resentment against Mormon encroachment on western lands led Brigham Young to recall his flock to Salt Lake. Cowan readied the farm to leave, but Eilley wanted to stay. She convinced Cowan she could hire men to work the farm while she tended to her boarders in Gold Canyon. Cowan returned to her periodically, but by August 1858 he left for good.

As more miners invaded Nevada's hills, Eilley built a new boardinghouse in the growing settlement of Gold Hill. One of her boarders, Lemuel Sanford "Sandy" Bowers, and his partner, James Rogers, owned a 20-foot mining claim in Gold Canyon. James "Old Virginny" Finney (who reputedly named the town of Virginia City) also owned mining interests in the area, as did drifter and sometime miner T. Henry Paige "Old Pancake" Comstock. Comstock boasted so often, and so loudly, that he was one of the first discovers of ore in Gold Canyon that when the gold and silver boom finally erupted, the area became known as the Comstock Lode.

Some of the first Comstock mining claims were recorded in a registration book supposedly kept on a shelf behind a bar in a local saloon. Sandy Bowers and James Rogers registered their holdings on January 28, 1859.

Gold Canyon veins finally started producing, yielding about $1,500 per ton of gold. When the first silver was extracted from the sticky mud that adhered to the gold deposits, the shiny ore proved to be worth twice as much—more than $3,000 a ton.

Between 1859 and 1890 the mines around Gold Canyon produced one of the largest strikes in history, with more than $400 million in gold and silver extracted from the hills. The communities that evolved from this bonanza—Gold Hill, Silver City, and Virginia City—became the central towns of the Comstock Lode.

Virginia City emerged as the most active community, boasting a population of better than 30,000 during the height of its prosperity. Precious ore seemed to seep out of the ground, bringing with it a menagerie of hastily erected tents and lean-to shacks, saloons, gambling halls, and brothels, along with an assortment of people from almost every part of the world. Men who had never seen more than $10 at one time now amassed fortunes overnight. No ground was left unturned beneath the shadow of Mount Davidson.

Eilley was not immune to the lure of riches, but stories vary as to how she acquired her own 10-foot claim. Some say one of her boarders, unable to pay his bill, gave her the deed to his mine as payment. But the old ledger on the saloon shelf indicated she paid $100 a foot for James Rogers's one-half interest in the claim he owned with Sandy Bowers. However she acquired it, Eilley and Sandy now owned adjoining claims. Over the ensuing years they would amass a fortune worth more than $4 million. Alison "Eilley" Bowers became the first woman millionaire on the Comstock.

On August 9, 1859, Eilley, now thirty-three, married twenty-six-year-old Sandy Bowers. She had not, however, divorced Alexander Cowan yet. Claiming desertion, she finalized the divorce on June 4, 1860, and was awarded one-half of the 320 acres she and Cowan owned in Washoe Valley.

On June 28, 1860, as the Bowerses' mines spewed forth thousands of dollars in ore, Eilley gave birth to a son, John Jasper Bowers. The elation of both Eilley and Sandy was short lived. Young John died on August 27, 1860.

The following year, Eilley found herself pregnant again. Possibly to celebrate the arrival of another child, a June 15, 1861, *Territorial Enterprise* article noted that ". . . Sandy Bowers had made his wife a present of one hundred tons of rock. Since then it has been crushed and has yielded $7000.00."

The day after the article appeared, so did little Theresa Fortunatas Bowers. The little girl died within three months, however, on September 17, 1861. Pioneer families suffered the loss of young children all too often. In its early years Nevada Territory enticed few doctors, and those who did come relied on limited knowledge and resources to aid the sick and injured. Quite possibly neither Bowers child ever saw a doctor. Eilley was left with empty arms after burying both her children in Gold Hill.

Maybe to ease the sorrow over the loss of their children, but more likely because they had more money than either had ever envisioned, the Bowers began building their mansion on Eilley's 160 acres in Washoe Valley.

While the house was under construction, the couple planned a grand European trip to purchase furnishings for their new home. On the evening of their departure from Virginia City, they hosted a magnificent banquet at the International Hotel, inviting the entire town to feast on an elaborate menu including free champagne. An unsophisticated Sandy addressed the crowd: "I've been in this yer country amongst the furst that come here. I've had powerful good luck, and I've got money to throw at the birds. . . . so me and Mrs. Bowers is agon' to Yoorop to take in the sights."

The Bowers left out of San Francisco on May 2, 1862, on the steamer *Golden Gate.* Arriving in England, Eilley looked forward to meeting Queen Victoria. She had a luxurious gown made for the occasion, a rich royal purple dress decorated with roses supposedly stitched in pure gold. Still, as hard and as often as she tried to see the queen, she was always rebuffed: Queen Victoria refused to see any divorced women. In recourse, Eilley is said to have taken ivy cuttings from Westminster Abbey that she carefully carried all the way back to Washoe Valley and planted around her mansion's veranda.

Eilley bought furniture in London. In Paris she purchased silverware, jewelry, and a vast wardrobe of dresses. The couple journeyed to Scotland for a reunion with Eilley's family. While there, she had a chair built out of rich walnut wood, stiff and formal, fit for a queen. They traveled to Italy and commissioned a Florence sculptor to create a series of statues. Only the heads, though; Eilley did not approve of the immodest full-body statues that lined the streets of Italy.

The Bowerses returned to Nevada in April 1863. When she got off the stage in Virginia City, Eilley held a baby girl in her arms. Speculation swirled like the Washoe zephyr winds as to where and how Eilley had acquired this child she called Margaret Persia Bowers. Though initially Margaret was thought to be Eilley's own daughter, born on the crossing to Europe, this story was never verified.

Another hypothesis claimed the child was born on board the returning ship to a Margaret Wixson, who subsequently died and was buried at sea. Eilley reportedly told the ship's captain she would search for the child's relatives when they docked, but when she failed to find them, she took the child to rear as her own. Yet another theory supposed Eilley adopted a Scottish-born child on the trip to her homeland. No proof exists for any of these assumptions, and Eilley never cared to disclose the truth.

Margaret Persia Bowers grew up in the newly constructed $400,000 Bowers Mansion, nestled in the foothills of towering Mount Rose. When Eilley first opened the doors of her mansion to greet Virginia City society, she eagerly anticipated the town clamoring to see the magnificent furnishings she had purchased in Europe. She was greatly disappointed.

Ill feeling against Mormons was still prevalent in Nevada; in addition, Eilley was a twice-divorced woman, something the good citizens of Virginia City refused to forgive. Later, as long as the liquor flowed and lavish meals satisfied their bellies, the elite of Virginia City accepted Eilley's hospitality and tolerated her display of unbridled wealth. But behind her back, they ridiculed the elaborate mansion as "Bowers' Folly."

By 1866 the Gold Canyon mines were playing out, and with the end of the Civil War, the country's need for massive amounts of ore declined. Eilley had never interfered with the management of the mines, relying on Sandy's abilities to assure that the money flowed as quickly as they both spent it. Unfortunately, Sandy had loaned thousands of dollars to anyone with a hand out. He'd mortgaged and sold their stock, and had even started negotiations to sell part of their holdings. To manage the mines more efficiently, he moved to Gold Hill to be on site, always assuming the next big strike was just a few feet away. Working tirelessly, he developed a cough that gave way to chills and fever.

On April 21, 1868, thirty-five-year-old Sandy Bowers died of silicosis, a lung disease prevalent in mining communities. Large amounts of dust from rocks found deep within the earth's crust suffocated unsuspecting miners. Eilley took Sandy's ashes back to Washoe Valley and buried them on a hill behind Bowers Mansion.

As the mining industry collapsed and her millions dwindled, Eilley still had a child to rear and a mansion that required thousands of dollars to maintain. An entrepreneurial woman, she determined her grand house could provide the money she and Margaret Persia needed. Charging admission, she organized dances and social events, advertising the hot springs as beneficial to invalids and the cool pools as relief on torrid summer days. She borrowed money to construct an addition that provided rooms for boarders as well as space for a dance hall.

An 1870 Carson City newspaper reported that for $5.00, one could enjoy such niceties at the Bowers Mansion as indoor bathrooms, a billiard room, and an expansive library. "The house itself is the most expensive and complete of any in Nevada, being furnished splendidly throughout. . . ."

Eilley finally realized she would have to sell the mines to pay off her ever-demanding creditors. The sale allowed her to keep the mansion for a while, but eventually she had to admit the place was too expensive to maintain. She urged the state to buy Bowers Mansion for use as an insane asylum, but the deal fell through.

To keep her creditors at bay and hold on to the mansion a while longer, she raffled off some of her possessions. For $2.50, one could buy a chance to own diamonds valued as high as $5,000.00, portraits by renowned artists, her valued silver service from Paris, furnishings and clothing from the grandest European shops. She continued to hold balls and parties; these brought in pittances that did little to appease her creditors.

Eilley had boarded Margaret Persia with friends in Reno so the child could attend school and to keep her away from the mansion's socials and sometimes raucous parties. There, on the night of July 14, 1874, Margaret Persia lay on her bed burning with fever. Eilley raced to her side, but her twelve-year-old daughter died before she arrived. Both scarlet fever and acute appendicitis were mentioned as possible causes of her death, but summer fevers were also sweeping through Reno that year, bringing typhoid, cholera, diphtheria, and malaria. Since vital records were not kept until 1887, the true cause of Margaret Persia's death remains a mystery.

Eilley took her last child home and buried her beside Sandy behind Bowers Mansion. Although she continued to hold gatherings at the house, her heart remained on the hill where her husband and daughter lay.

One of her largest and most successful parties occurred on June 26, 1875, when more than 4,000 members of the Pacific Coast Pioneers surged onto the lawns of Bowers Mansion for their Second Grand Outing. The Virginia & Truckee Railroad added twenty-two extra cars out of Reno for the event. An additional fifteen cars were coupled on at the Gold Hill station, two more in Silver City, and another in Carson City.

The party became a fitting sendoff for the grand mansion, for within the year Eilley's creditors finally lost patience. A sheriff's sale held at the Reno courthouse on May 3, 1876, finally divorced Eilley from her magnificent mansion. She had six months to settle the judgments against her before the sale became final, but she could not raise even the smallest amount to cover her debts. On November 27, 1876, Bowers Mansion passed out of her hands for good. Valued at $638,000 at the time of Sandy Bowers's death, Eilley's beloved mansion was wrested from her hands for a mere $10,000.

With no family and no means of support, Eilley took out her "peep stone" and set herself up in Virginia City as the Washoe Seeress, looking into the future for anyone willing to pay. She placed an ad in the *Territorial Enterprise* advertising her skills at clairvoyance:

MRS. L. S. BOWERS
THE FAMOUS WASHOE SEERESS!
Has returned to the Comstock and may be consulted at her residence, southwest corner of A street and Sutton Avenue, Virginia City. She will remain only about three weeks.

An 1878 *Territorial Enterprise* article promoted Eilley Bowers as "our own seeress," who "had a peculiar gift of some kind which enabled her to 'get out of herself' in some way and see and foretell curious things. . . . Better to consult those who have some reputation than to pay exorbitant prices to strolling humbugs."

A distraught woman asked Eilley to help locate a valuable ring. When Eilley envisioned it tossed in the trash, the woman looked and there was the ring. She told a carpenter not to go up on scaffolding, as it would collapse. He didn't go up and the scaffolding fell down. She supposedly predicted the devastating 1875 fire that destroyed large portions of Virginia City. She was not always successful with her messages, however; at one point she foretold a devastating earthquake, sending people scrambling to reinforce their homes and businesses. But the earth never shook.

As the population of Virginia City faded with the continuing decline of the mining industry, Eilley's business also waned. She moved to San Francisco in the 1880s and again advertised herself as a seeress. When she eventually returned to Nevada, her hearing had become so diminished she could not decipher the requests of her customers. Destitute, she relied on old friends to take her in, but finally ended up in the Washoe County poorhouse.

In 1900 Eilley wrote to everyone she knew asking for support in her claim against the government. She argued that she and Sandy had donated thousands of dollars to fight Indian wars as well as the Civil War, and she felt she deserved some of the money back to support her in her aging years. Ironically, her pleas for assistance fell on deaf ears.

By 1901 Nevada and California officials were arguing over who should assume the financial burden of providing care for Eilley. That August, Reno officials put her on a train for San Francisco with only $30 in her pocket. She lived at the King's Daughters Home in Oakland until her death on October 27, 1903, at the age of seventy-seven. Her ashes were eventually returned to Nevada and buried alongside her husband and daughter.

Alison "Eilley" Bowers left a legacy to the state of Nevada— her beloved Bowers Mansion in Washoe Valley. It stands today, about halfway between Reno and Carson City, as a monument to the woman who defied the mores of the day, divorced two men, made millions in the great Comstock bonanza, and designed, built, and furnished a house the likes of which had never been seen in Nevada. She outlived practically all the Comstock kings of fortune.

"Thus Nevada shakes off the responsibility of the destitute Washoe Seeress," lamented the *Nevada State Journal* when Eilley was discarded by the state. "Western hospitality, me-thinks, has taken unto itself wings and fled. But fare you well Mrs. Bowers, and our blessings (if nothing else) be with you."

FERMINIA SARRAS

1840–1915

Hard Rock Miner

The mound of gold coins spilled across the kitchen table, scattering onto the unstable wooden floor. Ferminia Sarras's dark Spanish eyes darted rapidly from coin to coin as she counted the riches before her. She may even have laughed aloud or danced a jig as she thought of the investors lining up to buy her mining claims. She was more than happy to negotiate away the years she had worked chipping out a living on hard rock and sterile soil in western Nevada. There were always men who would rather buy existing claims than dig their own fortunes.

She stopped ruminating through her treasure long enough to dwell on her plans for this pile of money—grand hotels, tables laden with sumptuous food, caches of jewelry, and wardrobes filled with fancy clothes—luxuries she sorely missed as she clamored up and down solid rock inclines in her dirty britches and worn-out boots. She couldn't wait to head for California and one of those ritzy hotels. She knew they would welcome her and her riches with open arms—and with luck some strong young man would do the same.

Gathering her loot, she hurried out the door of her shack and moved quickly along the barren path to an old chicken coop, disturbing a handful of hens in her wake. Stealthily, she hid her treasure amid the dirt and dung of the henhouse. Her nervous chickens would announce the approach of any thieves seeking to steal her stash, and she was more than willing and able to dissuade them from their mission.

When Ferminia Sarras first arrived in the Comstock area, she claimed to be a lady of royal Nicaraguan blood, and it's quite possible a conquistador or two was among her family's ancestors. Even the Esmeralda County, Nevada, tax office acknowledged her aristocratic status by listing her on the 1881 rolls as "Ferminia Sararis, Spanish Lady, Belleville." If she was not of noble heritage, she could certainly claim the wealth of royalty from the numerous mining claims she discovered during her thirty years seeking the myriad ores that lay beneath Nevada's rocky soil.

The Comstock, an area encompassing an assortment of small mining camps and newly formed towns such as Gold Hill and Virginia City, had no defined boundaries. Although gold and silver spewed from the hills around these two burgeoning communities, miners also sought ore deposits hundreds of miles from the original 1859 bonanza. Ferminia first appeared in Virginia City around 1880 but did not linger in the bawdy town. Instead, she headed into more remote areas to search for her ounce of gold. How a Spanish lady of royal blood acquired her knowledge of mining remains a mystery, as are many other aspects of Ferminia's life.

Born in Nicaragua in July 1840, her whereabouts are undocumented until her arrival in Virginia City. She must have created quite a stir when she showed up with her four daughters—Conchetta, the eldest; Concepción, age twelve; eight-year-old Juanita; and baby Emma, only five—with no sign of a husband. Although the children bore the last name *Flores*, no trace of their

Ferminia Sarras

father exists. Quite possibly, Ferminia, by this point forty years old, had left Nicaragua a widow, or her husband may have abandoned her and the girls in San Francisco where many immigrants first entered the United States. Ferminia never used the name *Flores*, although Nevada records over the years listed several spellings of her last name, from *Sararis* to *Serraras* to *Sararez*. Ferminia intermittently used both *Sarras* and *Sarrias*.

Ferminia Sarras was by no means the first woman miner to seek her fortune in Nevada. In 1871 a group of women combined their strength and talents to open a mine in Virginia City. Noting their endeavors, the *Territorial Enterprise* sided with the women's efforts to break through the barriers of this predominantly masculine occupation. "We do not see any reason why women should not engage in mining as well as men. If they can rock a cradle, they can run a car; if they can wash and scrub, they can pick and shovel."

Aware of the hardships she would encounter as she eked her fortune from unforgiving hills and the rock-hard desert earth, Ferminia left her two younger daughters, Juanita and toddler Emma, at an orphanage in Virginia City. She knew they would be watched over with greater care than she could provide.

With Conchetta and Concepción in tow, she headed more than 100 miles down the road from Virginia City to the Candelaria mining district. Silver had been discovered in Candelaria in 1864, and by the time Ferminia arrived, more silver was being taken out of the district than any other area of western Nevada.

Clusters of small mining sites dotted the Candelaria Hills, with settlements springing up wherever a handful of prospectors set up tents. The boroughs of Candelaria and Belleville were dubbed "good sporting towns," as saloons stayed open around the clock with nary a church in sight. Pickhandle Gulch acquired its name because fights often started and ended at the end of a pickax. Over the ensuing years Goldfield, Luning, Sodaville, and Santa Fe were established, branching out beyond the Candelaria Hills into the open desert.

Ferminia's presence in Candelaria, along with that of her two daughters, certainly stirred up emotions and a modicum of excitement, for women were a rarity in isolated mining outposts far from the bustle of Virginia City. Short and stout, yet bearing traces of her proud heritage, Ferminia's dark penetrating eyes, plus her agility with a gun, probably warned off unsuitable—and sometimes unsavory—men who approached her comely daughters. Yet Ferminia was the one who ultimately fell for the charms of a young Romeo, as became evident on January 25, 1881, when she gave birth to a son, Joseph A. Marshall.

No one stepped forward to claim Joseph as his son, although several men in the area bore the last name *Marshall*. Surely one would have wanted to boast of his conquest of the fiery Spanish lady.

Ferminia must have found this unexpected child troublesome; she lived a meager and often dangerous lifestyle, roaming from one promising outcrop to another, seeking elusive ores. She probably left baby Joseph to the care of daughter Concepción before heading out to climb the slippery, rock-strewn slopes and camp under the stars.

The Candelaria countryside was dry and desolate with nothing but greasewood, sagebrush, and bunchgrass thriving among volcanic rocks scattered across the desert floor. Historian Sally Zanjani, in her book *A Mine of Her Own: Women Prospectors in the American West, 1850–1950*, described the town as consisting of "a treeless, shadeless cluster of frame buildings, adobe huts, and tin-roofed dugouts in the hillsides. Nearly every day the wind blew, strongly enough to rip a shack from its foundations, an icy blast in winter, a breath from a fiery furnace in summer, coating everyone and everything in dust." Candelarians boasted the winters were so cold that beer and watery drinks froze—though "[n]one of the whiskey suffered, they don't water the liquor here."

Ferminia climbed the Candelaria Hills on winter days that brought chilling rains and snow along with the threat of frostbitten ears, fingers, and toes. During dry summer months, an unrelenting sun beat down upon her. How often did she resist drinking from toxic desert springs in which she could see the bony remains of those who had succumbed to their thirst? Did she dare take refuge in an ancient cave and risk disturbing a family of poisonous snakes or angry wolf pack? According to Zanjani, traveling light was not an option:

> She customarily went out on foot, wearing boots and pants and carrying a pack on her back. Few strapping male prospectors carried a pack over forty pounds, and Ferminia was no Amazon, being short and compactly built. But she was known for her remarkable strength, and in this desert country, where game and water were scarce, the prospector had to carry everything he might need. At a minimum, this included water, beans (the prospector's staple), dried fruit, the makings of sourdough bread or tortillas, a piece of canvas that could be used for bedding or a kind of hammock, a pick, an ax for firewood, a knife, and a frying pan. . . . Other more luxurious items, such as a coffeepot and cup, tin plate, extra clothes, and bedroll, were optional, and Ferminia had to leave plenty of room in her pack for the ore samples she carried out. Probably she also packed a gun, for wolves and packs of coyotes still roamed these hills, as well as men more dangerous than wolves.

Mining production reached its height in the Candelaria Hills from 1881 to 1883. ". . . [T]he people of Candelaria ate fresh strawberries and drank champagne," said Zanjani, "at the same time that hogs wandered through their shacks in search of scraps."

In April 1883 Ferminia staked her first claim, aptly calling it the Central American. She moved her family into a small house in the railroad town of Luning; by 1885 she had acquired a ranch in Sand Springs. She also purchased a toll road running through Tule Canyon into Death Valley, and the profit from this road often sustained her during the meager days of mining.

By this time daughter Conchetta had married; she would eventually have four children of her own before dying in 1893. Juanita, or Jennie as she now called herself, seventeen years old and no longer a ward of the state, had also married. She would have eight children, four of whom would not survive. The fate of little Emma has been lost to history.

Ferminia continued to roam the hills, staking the Amant and New Find claims in 1888, copper mines she uncovered near Luning. Her determination to find a big strike overwhelmed any need for comfort and companionship, and she seemed to thrive on this lonely existence. "So intoxicating was the promise of gold," said historian Ronald M. James, "that even when disappointed, the same people often followed the next call of a mineral bonanza."

By the mid-1890s the mines around Luning and Candelaria began to play out, and Ferminia moved farther south near Silver Peak in search of undiscovered outcroppings. She settled in a small adobe house and probably had to tighten her belt a few notches—as did many miners when the U.S. government ceased purchasing subsidies in Nevada silver mines. With the mining industry supporting the entire state, Nevada experienced a severe depression from about

1880 until the early 1900s, actually losing population during this time, the only western state to do so.

Ferminia realized small profits from the claims she owned around Luning, Candelaria, and Belleville, plus a scant income from the toll road in Tule Canyon. Often, destitute miners wandered into her camp or knocked on her door, knowing she was good for at least one decent meal and a place to sleep for a night or two. As soon as they were back on their feet, they left in search of the fortune that had so far eluded them, and she would soon follow their worn boot prints into the hills. Taunted for her unquenchable thirst for riches, she laughed off the cruel remarks, swearing her claims would outproduce all others in the county.

In 1895 fifty-five-year-old Ferminia claimed she had married Archie McCormack, a miner twelve years her junior. The union proved worthwhile according to a later *Los Angeles Times* story, which said she chose McCormack, and most of her other husbands and liaisons, for his strength and ability with a gun in warding off claim jumpers. Many of her paramours reportedly died violently while protecting her mining interests. McCormack died in a gunfight in 1906.

After working the Silver Peak district for more than ten years, Ferminia finally admitted defeat and abandoned her interests without finding the strike she knew was so near. Settling in the Santa Fe area, she registered a handful of claims throughout that summer while Joseph, now eighteen years old, worked nearby as a cowboy.

The new century began with a roar when lucrative ore deposits were uncovered in the booming town of Tonopah in 1900, lifting the entire state out of its economic depression. Ferminia couldn't get the ore out of the hills fast enough as her claims soared in value. Her penchant for finding copper seemed to outweigh her talent for discovering gold and silver. Investors clamored to her door, cash in hand, to purchase her holdings. She agreed to sell twenty-five of her claims for $8,000 each, with $20 gold pieces her preferred form of payment; this may have been the money strewn across her kitchen table. Although she received only a down payment on this fortune, it was still enough to allow her to become a lady again. Her great-grandson Albert Bradshaw once told Zanjani:

> She kind of liked the other side of life too, you know, the nice side, the good side, the fancy side. So she'd go to L.A. or San Francisco, preferably San Francisco and she'd get the finest hotel there was, and go out and buy the finest clothes there was, shoes, hat, dresses—the whole act. And dine and wine and everything, just right up to the first class. . . . She would hire a limousine and a chauffeur, and if she got a little bit lonesome, why she'd go out and get a gigolo, and they'd go out and have a big party, and have a good time.

When the money and men ran out, she would sell her fancy clothes and return to Nevada to climb the hills once more.

By 1905 the Goldfield and Tonopah districts needed a railroad depot to accommodate the flood of ore-seeking miners, businessmen, and potential settlers flocking into the area. The two towns were also supply points for freight hauled to and from multiple mining communities. Although the town of Sodaville was the obvious choice for a station, a local speculator, gambling that the railroad would establish the depot there, bought up most of the land, then demanded an exorbitant price for his holdings.

Recoiling at paying his unreasonable charges, the railroad chose instead to create a new town just north of the Candelaria Hills where Ferminia had first started her quest for Nevada's precious minerals. Since she was already known as the queen of copper for her success in mining the blue-green ore, plus owning some of the most productive mines in the area, the railroad chose to honor her by naming the new town Mina.

It wasn't long after Mina was established that a Boston syndicate showed interest in some of Ferminia's claims, and she was ready and willing to sell for the right price. As the shadows of autumn crept across the arid soil of Candelaria in 1905, she closed the deal on forty of her claims for a total of $90,000. After depositing a stash of gold coins in her chicken coop bank, she again headed for San Francisco and the lights and loves that awaited her.

Two years later a San Francisco brokerage firm offered her $65,000 for more of her claims, and she was off on another San Francisco trip. Champagne flowed like water, and she never tired of ordering trays of food laden with fresh fish, prime cuts of beef, and lavish desserts. Jewelry, furs, and trunks of clothing were more than likely delivered right to her hotel room from shops eager to share in Ferminia's wealth. And then there were the men. She preferred her escorts young and fit, capable of keeping up with her active lifestyle. There were plenty of men in California willing to give it a try.

Saloons from Tonopah to Reno speculated on how much the first lady of Mina was worth. Even though she sold off many of her claims, she still had dozens of producing mines. The Jennie and Dolly Emma mines were named for her daughters, as was the Joseph for her son. The Archie was probably named for Archie McCormack. The Nelly, Salley, and Luesa claims might have been names of women she met as she traveled from one small mining camp to another. But most of her claims were named for men— the Harry, Bill Thomas, Johnny Bull, Frank, Bill Engles, and Tom Moro. The Whiskey and Brandy mines need no explanation.

By 1909 mining in the dry, remote Candelaria Hills began to fade when larger, more lucrative copper strikes were discovered farther east near Ely, Nevada. Approaching seventy years of age and no longer able to climb the hills as she used to, Ferminia settled in Luning near her son Joseph, who was now married and following his mother's quest for gold, silver, copper—anything that would yield the same riches she had uncovered. Daughter Jennie, divorced and remarried, lived in nearby Goldfield. Seven-year-old Tom, one of Jennie's sons, was sent to live with his grandmother, keeping her company on long summer nights, listening to her tales of fortunes found and treasures lost.

As evidenced by her stash in the chicken coop, Ferminia never trusted banks, but for some reason, when she sold a handful of claims in 1914, she deposited the funds in a Los Angeles bank. She may have been influenced by her latest love, Domingo Velasco, at least thirty years her junior. Unfortunately, this time her penchant for younger men proved her undoing. Velasco had his eye on a much younger woman, and once he'd extracted Ferminia's cash from the Los Angeles bank, he and his sweetheart fled to South America, never to be seen again. Newspapers headlined her plight, claiming she'd lost thousands of dollars to Velasco. Ferminia made one last, fruitless trip to California in search of the young Lothario.

Desolate and alone, she returned to Luning never to scour the hills again for elusive ores. Seventy-five-year-old Ferminia Sarras died in early February 1915 and was buried in Luning. The *Western Nevada Miner* hailed her as "one of the last of those brave spirits who dared the desert's fierce glare in Nevada's primitive days and blazed the trails that others might follow." Another newspaper called her "one of the most remarkable characters the gold regions ever produced."

In a will she signed shortly before her death, Ferminia named only a handful of family members as beneficiaries of her estate. Even then, those named received their shares only if they continued to work her mines. Although she spent money as if her rickety kitchen tabletop would always be covered with $20 gold pieces, she was still a wealthy woman when she died.

Her family believed she had married once again shortly before her death. Mexican-born Fermine Arriaga, thirty-five years younger than Ferminia, might have expected a substantial reward for marrying a lonely old woman, but when the terms of her will became known, he received nothing. Enraged, he swore he would "cut the gold teeth from her mouth."

No one knows what happened to the stash of gold coins secreted in the old chicken coop. She might have spent it all or carried it into the mountains for safekeeping; maybe someone finally found a way around the protective hens and stole it. Or is it still there? With the death of the last family member who knew where the ramshackle henhouse stood, the location remains a mystery.

Ferminia Sarras represents hundreds of women miners who endured Nevada's early mining years, only to have their names and faces forgotten by historians and history writers. Only recently have the lives of some of these women become known. So many walked those lonely miles alone, sometimes afraid but never without the talent and ability to take pickax in hand and dig out the gems that lay buried beneath the Nevada desert.

Quotes from *A Mine of Her Own: Women Prospectors in the American West, 1859–1950* by Sally Zanjani reprinted by permission of the University of Nebraska Press. © 1997 by the University of Nebraska Press.

SARAH WINNEMUCCA HOPKINS

1844–1891

A Sparrow Among Eagles

In 1864 twenty-year-old Sarah Winnemucca, a Paiute Indian, stood on the stage of Henry Sutliffe's Music Hall in Virginia City as the audience rose, their applause thundering in an avalanche of praise. She nervously brushed her hands against her buckskin skirt, the swaying fringe revealing ornately beaded boots. Long, coal-black hair fell across delicate features as she turned to smile at her father, Chief Winnemucca, who stood stoically behind her.

Sarah and her father hoped their presentation would mend escalating tensions between white Nevada settlers and the Northern Paiute Indians, as well as garnering enough food and clothing to keep the Paiutes from starving or freezing that winter. It was the beginning of a journey that would leave Sarah heartbroken, destitute, and ill as she attempted time and again to bring understanding and cooperation between two very different cultures. Not until long after her death would she be heralded as a peacemaker between the two races.

Sarah Winnemucca's birth the summer of 1844 near the Humboldt River occurred just prior to the great influx of gold seekers crossing the desert plains to California. Captain Truckee, the Paiute chief and Sarah's grandfather, served as guide for parties heading west and considered the white man his friend and peer.

Her parents, Winnemucca and Tuboitony, named Sarah *Thocmetony*, meaning "shell flower." She spent her childhood beside her mother and other Paiute women and children traveling miles each day gathering roots, herbs, and wild seeds to flavor the fish, ground squirrels, and larger game caught by the men. Crunchy delicacies of roasted crickets and grasshoppers were favorite treats. Although they considered the Pyramid Lake region their homeland, the Paiutes were hunters and gatherers, not settling to farm but preferring to rely on the land for sustenance.

The Paiutes kept their past alive by relating ancient tales. The story of Cannibal Owl, who snatched naughty children, pounded them into pulp, and ate them, is a typical legend. When her father described the first white men he saw as owl-like with scraggly gray beards and colorless, ghostly eyes, Sarah steadfastly believed she would be eaten if caught by one of these white apparitions.

Sometimes nightmares become reality. As white miners and settlers penetrated farther into their territory, Sarah's people learned to avoid the newcomers—encounters usually ended in tragedy for the unsophisticated Paiutes. One terrifying incident cemented Sarah's fear of the white intruders.

Sara's mother, Tuboitony, and the other women were gathering seeds when a band of white men approached. As Tuboitony ran, little Sarah and her cousin lagged behind, unable to keep up with the fleeing adults. Rather than endanger the entire band, Tuboitony dug a trench in the sandy soil and ordered the two little girls into the ditch. She pushed dirt atop them and spread sagebrush over their heads to protect them from the sun. She then fled, leaving the girls to their fate. The sun rose higher and hotter before starting its westward descent toward a darkness filled with

Sarah Winnemucca Hopkins circa 1883–1890

unknown terrors. Would the white men find them, smacking their lips as they stoked a roaring fire before pounding them to death? Or would marauding coyotes discover them first? Suddenly the girls heard rustling in the bushes and knew their fate was but a few feet away. In her book *Life Among the Paiutes: Their Wrongs and Claims,* Sarah described what happened next:

> At last we heard some whispering. We did not dare to whisper to each other, so we lay still. I could hear their footsteps coming nearer and nearer. I thought my heart was coming out of my mouth. Then I heard my mother say, "T is right here!" Oh, can any one in this world ever imagine what were my feelings when I was dug up by my poor mother and father?

Captain Truckee ruled the Northern Paiutes wisely and compassionately. Having guided the whites into California, he understood they would soon wield more power than his people could ever muster. In 1851 he took a contingent of Paiutes to California to learn the white man's ways. Six-year-old Sarah, convinced she would be eaten by the dreaded white owls, cowered under a blanket as they crossed the Nevada plains.

After returning to their homeland, Winnemucca and Tuboitony sent Sarah and her younger sister Elma to live with Major William Ormsby, who ran a stage depot in Genoa, then part of Utah Territory. The Ormsbys taught the girls to speak and write English. In return, Sarah and Elma worked in the depot store, helped with household chores, and were companions for little Lizzie Anne Ormsby. The Ormsbys' kindness toward the two girls during the year they lived with them alleviated some of Sarah's doubts about white savages. It may have been during this time that

Thocmetony acquired her English name of Sarah and her sister became known as Elma.

By the winter of 1858, the influx of white settlers had devastated the vast herds of wild game, fish, plants, and seeds that the Paiutes relied upon for sustenance. As bitter winds howled and snow drifted to towering heights, the Paiutes were forced to ask for assistance from Virginia City citizens—warm clothing and enough food to make it through the winter. But their pleas were ignored, and many froze or starved to death. The following winter brought little relief and even colder temperatures.

Old Captain Truckee, perhaps sensing his pending death, requested that Winnemucca and Tuboitony send Sarah and Elma to school in California to learn about the new world emerging around them. The San Jose school seemed amicable to the girls, but after only a few weeks white parents objected to their children sitting next to the Indians and insisted they leave.

White settlers, prospectors, and businesses now dominated the West. Virginia City boasted a white population of almost 15,000, and they wanted the Paiutes off the lush, productive land surrounding Pyramid Lake. The Natives were already restricted in where they could hunt and fish. Now the white populace wanted to determine where the Indians could live, pledging to provide food, clothing, and farming equipment if the Indians would stay within proscribed reservation boundaries. None of these promises materialized.

Winnemucca, now tribal leader after Captain Truckee's death, took the plight of his people to the citizens of Nevada. He walked onto the stage of Sutliffe's Music Hall that day in 1864 with Sarah, Elma, son Natches, and a handful of other Paiutes seeking assistance from the people of Virginia City. Sarah interpreted her father's words for the audience.

The Paiute group continued on to San Francisco and made their plea before an audience at the Metropolitan Theater. Sarah donned the expected attire—buckskin skirt trimmed with fringe and ornately beaded boots. She had quickly assessed the delight of white audiences when she romanticized her appearance, dressing as writers depicted Indians in western dime novels rather than in more traditional attire. Though the troupe was well received in San Francisco, their appeals were largely ignored.

In 1865, when Chief Winnemucca and his men were on a hunting expedition, a cavalry troop rode into the Paiute camp and accused the Indians of stealing cattle and slaying two white men. Refusing to believe the Indians' denial, the cavalry slaughtered thirty women, children, and old men. Sarah's sister Mary fled to the mountains to warn Chief Winnemucca and his men not to return. By the time the Mud Lake Massacre was over, Mary and Sarah's mother, Tuboitony, lay dead.

Conditions on Pyramid Lake Reservation became unbearable. The Paiutes were desperate for food and clothing. Tempers flared between the two races.

The summer of 1868 brought no relief for the destitute Paiutes. Sarah and Natches went to Camp McDermit near the Oregon border seeking assistance from the army. Recognizing her ability to speak several languages—English, Spanish, and various Indian dialects—the army hired Sarah as an interpreter. Natches, with the promise of protection and provisions for his people, was sent to bring in Chief Winnemucca. That July, around 500 Paiutes chose to relocate to Camp McDermit rather than starve to death.

Sarah believed her people could become productive farmers if taught how to plow and sow, skills they had not needed as hunters and gatherers. In a letter to Ely Samuel Parker, commissioner of

Indian affairs, she offered her solution to the problem of feeding her people and respecting their needs:

> So far as their knowledge of agriculture extends they are quite ignorant as they never had an opportunity of learning but I think if proper pains were taken that they would willingly make the effort to maintain themselves by their own labor if they could be made to believe that the products were to be their own and for their own use and comfort.

Nothing came of her request for assistance, so in 1870 Sarah returned to San Francisco, where newspapers touted her as "Princess Sarah." But once again, false promises and undelivered goods were all the Paiutes received.

While she was still at Camp McDermit, First Lieutenant Edward D. Bartlett caught Sarah's eye with his dashing uniform, expert horsemanship, and happy-go-lucky lifestyle. Marriages between Native Americans and whites were forbidden in Nevada, so the couple traveled to Salt Lake City and wed on January 29, 1871. Unbeknown to Sarah, Bartlett had deserted his company. His fun-loving nature seemed to need the nourishment of copious amounts of liquor, purchased with money acquired by pawning Sarah's jewelry without her knowledge. The marriage was over within the year, although not legally dissolved until 1876.

In 1872 the Paiutes were relocated to the Malheur Reservation about 80 miles north of Camp McDermit. Resident Indian agent Sam Parrish and his wife were well liked, never demeaning the Paiutes' customs or needs; they also paid fair wages for work. When Mrs. Parrish opened a school, she and Sarah taught side by side. Under the supervision of Agent Parrish, the Paiutes accepted the confines of reservation living.

Unfortunately, life does not continue along straight and serene courses. Sam Parrish, never much of a religious man, was soon relieved of his duties, because the law insisted reservations be under Christian leadership. His replacement, former army officer W. V. Rinehart, bore ill will toward the Paiutes and soon ran afoul of the determined Sarah.

Rinehart blamed all the problems he encountered at Malheur on Sarah's insistent requests for fair treatment of the Paiutes. He refused to pay them for work they performed and withheld much-needed food and clothing. He closed Mrs. Parrish's school. Rinehart claimed Sarah was disloyal and purposely stirred up trouble. He threatened to put her in prison but, instead, banished her from the reservation.

In June 1878 a contingent of neighboring Paiutes begged Sarah to help their starving families. "You are our only voice," they pleaded. Realizing that assistance had to come from the highest power of the land, she decided to go to Washington, DC.

Sarah made it as far as the Oregon–Idaho border, where the Bannock tribe, as destitute as the Paiutes, rallied against their oppressive Indian agent. With war pending, Sarah returned to her people.

Chief Winnemucca refused to join the Bannock uprising. In retaliation, the Bannocks held him and a contingent of his band hostage. When Sarah learned that her father was behind enemy lines, she vowed to bring her people to safety, offering her services as interpreter and scout to General O. O. Howard, commander during the Bannock War. Along with her brother Lee and his wife, Mattie, she set out across miles of treacherous, rocky terrain to rescue the Paiute prisoners, stopping only for fresh horses before heading out again. Nearing the Bannock stronghold, they quit their horses and, on hands and knees, crawled up the side of the mountain.

Peering into the enemy camp, they found the Bannocks butchering cattle for an evening feast. The shadowy figures stealthily maneuvered their way through enemy lines to the imprisoned Paiutes, then led seventy-five of their people to safety. Over a three-day period, the triad rode more than 200 rough miles to bring the Paiutes home.

Sarah continued to serve under General Howard as interpreter and scout during the Bannock War, slipping in and out of enemy camps, stealing plans, intercepting Bannock war signals, and aiding in the capture of Bannock warriors.

After one particularly bloody fight, soldiers found a Bannock baby on the ground covered in dirt. The little girl was turned over to Sarah and Mattie, but knowing they could not care for the baby and continue to scout for the army, they entrusted her to two Bannock women prisoners. After the war, Sarah found the child's parents and reunited the family. The grateful couple named their daughter Sarah for her rescuer.

Sarah and Mattie were often called upon to hunt down fleeing Bannock prisoners. During one escapade across rock-hard ground, Mattie's horse slipped and tossed her brutally to the earth. Her injuries were severe, and Sarah feared for her sister-in-law's life.

By August 1878 the Bannock War was over. Because the Paiutes had not joined the hostile Bannocks, they assumed they would be allowed to stay at Malheur Reservation. The army, however, considered all Indians prisoners of war regardless of tribe. The Paiutes were ordered to Yakima Reservation in Washington Territory, a distance of more than 350 miles over treacherous mountain ranges. They would travel in the middle of winter clad in threadbare blankets and worn-out boots.

On January 6, 1879, fifty wagons started out across the mountains of Oregon and Washington. Elderly Paiutes froze to death and were left beside the road; children died in their parents' arms. Sarah watched a mother and her new baby die. Mattie struggled against unconsciousness in the back of a roughshod wagon.

The Paiutes were promised warm clothing, an abundance of food, and comfortable lodgings at the end of their journey. What greeted them after almost a month on the hard, bitter road was a hastily built, unheated 150-foot shed that let in cold winter winds and drifting snow. Firewood was nonexistent, and scant food was provided to the already emaciated group. The Paiutes were assured that wagonloads of warm clothing were on the way. With spring came the promised goods: twenty-eight shawls and a handful of fabrics. Everything else had been sold to the highest bidder before reaching the Indians. Mattie died at the end of May.

Sarah taught school at Yakima, but as soon as she received her pay from the army for her scouting and interpreting duties, she set out again for Washington, DC. She was determined to secure aid for her people and to return them to Pyramid Lake. Her route was circuitous.

In November 1879 she went to see General Howard, who had not forgotten her invaluable help during the Bannock War. He gave her a letter of introduction to Washington officials. Stopping next in San Francisco, where her heroic deeds during the war had made her a celebrity, she took the opportunity to speak at Platte's Hall. She told of her people's history, how Captain Truckee had welcomed white settlers and led them across the Nevada desert to the gold fields of California. She recounted the treatment received at the hands of Indian agents such as W. V. Rinehart, and then she detailed the horrible march to Yakima.

An 1879 article in the *San Francisco Chronicle* recognized Sarah's stamina and poise:

> Sarah has undergone hardships and dared dangers
> that few men would be willing to face, but she

never lost her womanly qualities. . . . She speaks
with force and decision, and talks eloquently of
her people. Her mission, undertaken at the request
of Chief Winnemucca, is to have her tribe gathered together again at their old home in Nevada,
where they can follow peaceable pursuits and
improve themselves.

Chief Winnemucca, Natches, and a cousin joined her on her
trek to Washington, DC. There they met Carl Schurz, secretary of
the interior, who promised to send supplies and suggested they
return home to await the glut of provisions that would be forthcoming. Before leaving the capital of freedom, they toured the
White House, where they met President Rutherford B. Hayes.

Yet Sarah's nemesis, Agent Rinehart, had already laid the
foundation for her defeat in Washington by sending a barrage of
letters to E. A. Hayt, commissioner of Indian affairs, disparaging
her character, calling her a woman of low means, and accusing her
of prostitution. Schurz may have become aware of Rinehart's accu-
sations, for he reneged on his promises to send provisions to the
destitute Indians.

Failing once again to obtain aid, Sarah's loyalty came under
question by her own people. She had traveled between two diverse
worlds for so long, experiencing the harsh existence of reservation life along with the comforts enjoyed in white settlements.
Some of her people felt she had sold out for a more lucrative
lifestyle.

Once again Sarah tried to find companionship and love in the
arms of a white man. Fair-haired Virginian Lewis H. Hopkins, like
Edward Bartlett, liked the action of gambling halls and saloons.
Although he was five years younger than Sarah, the couple married
in San Francisco on December 5, 1881.

The newlyweds enjoyed little wedded bliss. When Chief Winnemucca died in 1882, Sarah's brother Natches became Paiute chief, and she was once again asked to intercede on the tribe's behalf. She and Hopkins traveled east in 1883. On this trip Sarah met two sisters, Elizabeth Palmer Peabody and Mary Mann.

Elizabeth Peabody, considered the first woman book publisher in the United States, also owned a bookstore frequented by the literary elite of Boston. She arranged a series of lectures for Sarah, encouraging her to detail the history and culture of the Paiute people, to explain to America that the Indians had no land, no citizenship, and no government representation.

Elizabeth then urged Sarah to write down the history of the Paiutes. Sarah considered herself a poor writer but Mary Mann, widow of educator Horace Mann, offered to edit her work. The commingling of three compassionate hearts and minds resulted in Sarah's book *Life Among the Paiutes: Their Wrongs and Claims*, published in 1883 and thought to be the first book written by a Native American woman.

On April 22, 1884, Sarah spoke before Congress, petitioning for an allotment of land for her people at Pyramid Lake. Although Interior Secretary Schurz opposed the action, a bill was passed on July 6, 1884, giving each family 160 acres of Nevada land. It was not good land—that had been gobbled up by white settlers—but at least they would be back on home soil.

While Sarah counted on the money she received from her lectures and the sale of her book to provide funds for her people, Lewis Hopkins preferred to gamble away a good portion of her earnings. Very little was left by the time they returned to Nevada.

With her scant savings, plus the financial help of Elizabeth Peabody and Mary Mann, Sarah opened the Peabody Institute—a school in Lovelock, Nevada. She had always believed that education would bridge the disparities between the races, and said so in an article in the *Winnemucca Silver State* newspaper in 1886:

> It seems strange to me that the Government has not found out years ago that education is the key to the Indian problem. Much money and many precious lives would have been saved if the American people had fought my people with Books instead of Power and lead. Education civilized your race and there is no reason why it cannot civilize mine.

When Mary Mann died, she bequeathed her small estate to Sarah to help run the Peabody Institute. Sarah managed to keep the school open for a while but was soon inundated with financial woes. With her physical and emotional strength weakening, she was finally forced to close the establishment in 1888.

Ill, tired, and discouraged, Sarah went to live with her sister Elma at Henry's Lake on the Montana–Idaho border.

Sarah died in October 1891. She was only forty-seven years old. Although exhausted from years of fighting for her people, she had never quit. Her own words expressed her determination to return the Paiutes to the land of their ancestors: "When I think of my past life, and the bitter trials I have endured, I can scarcely believe I live, and yet I do; and, with the help of Him who notes the sparrow's fall, I mean to fight for my down-trodden race while life lasts."

DAT SO LA LEE
?–1925

Washoe Basket Weaver

*I*n 1978 four highly valued Washoe Indian baskets and a handful of arrowheads disappeared from the Nevada Historical Society Museum in Reno. The thief or thieves managed to grab the baskets from their display cases—each basket measured about 12 by 15 inches—and leave the building without being detected.

Two years later one basket was recovered in California and returned to the museum for a finder's fee of $2,500. In 1998 an art dealer in Tucson, Arizona, having procured three Washoe baskets, sent them to an appraiser in California. Not recognizing the baskets, the appraiser forwarded photos of them to an expert in British Columbia for attribution. Suddenly the Federal Bureau of Investigation was on the art dealer's doorstep in Tucson, wanting to know from whom and where he had purchased the baskets. The art dealer had no idea the baskets were stolen goods and voluntarily turned them over to the FBI. He was not charged with the theft and received $55,000 for returning them, the sum he had originally paid for the baskets.

The FBI turned the three baskets over to the Reno Historical Society to assure they would be properly cared for while agents

Dat so la lee

continued their investigation. Reportedly, when the director of the historical society flew to Arizona to retrieve the baskets, he refused to put his treasured cargo in the baggage hold of the airplane for the return trip. Instead he purchased three additional airline seats so they would not leave his sight until back where they belonged. No one was ever charged with the theft of the baskets, which were said to be worth between $150,000 and $300,000 each.

How did a Canadian art expert, so far from the scene of the crime, recognize these valuable baskets? Dr. Marvin Cohodas of the University of British Columbia knew exactly who had created the three hundred-year-old baskets. As an authority on Washoe Indian basketry, he had no trouble recognizing the work of the woman who is recognized as the most renowned Washoe basket weaver—Dat so la lee. Where the baskets had been since their removal from the Reno Historical Society Museum twenty years previously remains a mystery even today. The life of Dat so la lee is also somewhat of a mystery.

Born around the mid-1800s, Dat so la lee lived in and around the Carson Valley area and into the Sierra Nevadas, never far from beautiful Lake Tahoe. The Washoe (also spelled *Washo*) had neither chiefs nor leaders. Relying on the land for sustenance, they preferred to gather seeds, fish, and hunt wild rabbit and deer rather than farm the land. They never acquired horses to travel great distances. For the most part they lived peacefully with their neighbors, the Pomo and Maidu Indians in eastern California, and the Paiutes along the western border of what would eventually become the state of Nevada. Of the four main Nevada tribes—the Northern Paiute, Southern Paiute, Shoshone, and Washoe—the Washoe were the smallest in number. All these indigenous clans traded among each other, with the Washoe refining their talents as basket makers by incorporating the methods and intricacies of other tribes.

Washoe women made simple, unadorned baskets to hold the seeds and acorns they collected. Baskets lined with pitch held water. They cooked food by dropping a series of hot rocks into baskets filled with liquid, meat, and vegetables, then constantly moved the baskets back and forth to prevent them from burning. When the rocks cooled, they were replaced until the food was thoroughly cooked.

Little is known of Dat so la lee's childhood but, like all the Washoe, she certainly watched as white settlers spread across her native land. The rabbits and deer disappeared. Grass seeds and acorns, staples of the Washoe diet, vanished under the stampede of cattle and sheep or lay buried beneath the plow of industrious farmers. The Washoe became servants of the white populace in growing towns and campsites. They cooked, washed clothes, tended white children, and helped till the land, all for food they could no longer provide for themselves.

Dat so la lee learned the intricacies of making baskets, as did all young Washoe girls. When white settlers brought out their iron pots for cooking, however, many women abandoned ancient basket-weaving practices. Why spend days, sometimes months, creating a container that lasted only a few years when a big heavy pot did the same job and lasted almost forever? Few Washoe women continued to create the willow masterpieces. Many forgot their talents.

In the late 1800s Dat so la lee married Assu and had two children, neither of whom lived to adulthood. When Assu died, she may have married again, but there is little evidence of that union. She worked around Carson Valley washing the clothes of white settlers and tending to their children. And unlike most of her contemporaries, she continued to make baskets. Around 1888 she married master arrow craftsman Charley Keyser, part Washoe and twenty-four years her junior. At the same time, she took the American name Louisa Keyser—the third name she had acquired in her short lifetime.

When Dat so la lee was born, she received the name Dabuda, probably from her father, Da da u on ga la. When asked years later, she did not know her mother's name, and it's quite possible her mother died in childbirth. *Dabuda* may mean "young willow" in the Washoe language, certainly a fitting title for the yet-to-be celebrated weaver of baskets.

Around 1895 Dat so la lee was working as a laundress for Abram and Amy Cohn, second-generation owners of The Emporium, a clothing store in Carson City. The Cohns bought baskets from Indian tribes throughout the Southwest and California to sell alongside broad-brimmed hats, boots, and petticoats. When Abe saw the baskets his washerwoman wove in her spare time, he recognized her talent and encouraged her to spend more hours weaving and less time cleaning his clothes. Realizing that she might be his ticket to wealth and fame, he made her a proposition no poor Indian woman could ignore: In exchange for weaving her baskets solely for his store, he would provide her and Charley with a home, food, clothing, and medical care. Dat so la lee and Charley accepted Abe's offer, and a cloak of mystery fell over Dat so la lee's life.

The Cohns mastered the art of mythmaking, creating a fictional figure out of an ordinary Indian woman who only wanted to earn enough money to support herself and her husband. They wove stories of intrigue and romanticism around Dat so la lee and her unique form of basket weaving, hoping to entice more customers into their store.

Dat so la lee's baskets were derived from a combination of Washoe traditional weavings and Pomo Indian basketry. Her invention of the *degikup* (pronounced *day-gee-coop*) basket—a finely coiled container that started with a small, round bottom, ballooned in the middle, and then returned to a small opening at the top of equal size to the bottom—is considered to have renewed interest in Washoe basketry. This design gave her baskets a three-dimensional appearance. The word *degikup* refers to the small mouth-shaped rim.

She started each basket with a three-rod foundation made of willow twigs. She then sewed or wove around the foundation with simple, finely coiled stitches, measuring about twenty-five stitches per inch. Most of her baskets were finished in a self-rim with tapered stitches.

The background of her baskets was crafted from strips of pale-colored willow found just beneath the bark. Black stitching came from mature, brown fern roots that were dug up in spring, then buried in mud for several weeks until they turned black. In summer red bark was stripped from bunch trees, creating the red coloring of her designs. All these materials took days to dry, then were shredded and curled before curing. Lastly, they were cut into narrow strips ready to be woven into designs created from Dat so la lee's imagination. Some of her baskets took more than a year to complete.

Abe Cohn falsely claimed Dat so la lee acquired the *degikup* form of basketry from her ancestors—that this particular style was hers alone by family right. He also said she was the daughter of a chief and that the design on one of her baskets depicted the different levels of Washoe leadership, even though the Washoe did not subscribe to any form of hierarchy. According to Cohn, other weavers were forbidden to copy her style of basketry, and Washoe law deemed she could not weave the same design twice.

In actuality, Dat so la lee was the innovator and creator of the *degikup* style of basketry, and she often used the same design on different baskets. After 1900, as her construction techniques and designs grew in popularity, other basket weavers imitated her work. They wove to satisfy the demand for attractive, salable baskets, not to replicate ancient designs and imagery. Coloring was added to make the baskets more appealing to buyers and traders. Today the *degikup* basket is considered one of the most collectible forms of early Indian basketry.

Although Abe Cohn is credited with establishing Dat so la lee as a master basket weaver, Amy Cohn was the real creator of the Indian woman's fictional history. Amy wrote stories and gave lectures touting the intricacies of Dat so la lee's weaving, adding greatly to the myth surrounding the heavyset woman. Disregarding Dat so la lee's obesity, Amy invented a tale about her and Charley traipsing up and down the hillsides gathering tree limbs, roots, and bark to construct her unique baskets. She manufactured another story describing Dat so la lee sitting for hours splitting willow fibers with her teeth and fingernails, then smoothing the resulting threads with a piece of glass. "All day she sits patiently weaving these strands in-and-out," one of Amy's brochures read, "taking many moons to finish one of her rare and valuable *day-gee-coops*, or ceremonial baskets."

Sometimes Dat so la lee did sit in the window of The Emporium while passersby watched her interweave bundles of stripped willow and bark. Carson City newspapers announced the completion of each new *degikup* basket.

Amy invented stories about the baskets, giving them ritual significance even though they had none. She kept a ledger for each basket, indicating the date started and finished, a description of the design crafted on the basket, and the occasion for which it was made. All were numbered and titled. Statistics listed dimension, weight, and materials used. Even the weaving technique and stitch count were recorded. For years this ledger was the standard against which traders judged the value of Washoe baskets.

The Cohns sought to depict Dat so la lee as a product of the era before white settlers altered the Washoe lifestyle, before indigent

Indians begged for handouts on the streets of Carson City. They wanted to present the image of a naive Native maiden working at her ancient craft; they believed this was what the white public wanted to see, not the reality of Washoe poverty. To give Dat so la lee a more romantic history, they changed her birth date by at least ten years, claiming that she was old enough to be one of the first Washoe to meet explorer John C. Frémont—considered the first white man to see the tribe in 1844.

Yet for all the liberties the Cohns took with Dat so la lee's life, they must be credited with bringing her basketry to the forefront of public attention, making her talent renowned among collectors worldwide. Abe and Amy Cohn freed the Indian artist from working menial jobs, encouraging her to create her legendary baskets and leave a legacy of artistry.

Dat so la lee really didn't need anyone to create a fantasy about her life or her ability to create magnificent baskets. And even though she was an uneducated Indian woman who signed her name with the palm of her hand, by the beginning of the twentieth century she far outshone other basket weavers in artistic ability.

In the summer of 1900, Amy took Dat so la lee to Tahoe City to display her baskets. That August she sought to expand her customer base by taking Dat so la lee to the California State Fair in San Francisco. And in September the Cohns and Dat so la lee exhibited baskets at the Nevada State Fair in Reno. Wherever they went, the big Indian woman attracted attention. Her fame was beginning to equal her size.

In 1903, in an effort to capitalize on an increasing national interest in western art, Amy opened a shop, the Biscoe, in Tahoe City. Every summer until her death, she took Dat so la lee to Lake Tahoe, where the big woman sat outside the store weaving.

Although Amy was socially active in Carson City, most of her time was spent in the company of Dat so la lee. The two women must have formed a sisterly bond on some level during the years they spent together. They traveled extensively in each other's company and certainly shared some moments of intimacy. Over the years Dat so la lee wove a set of miniature baskets, which she gave to Amy for her personal collection.

As the decades passed and Dat so la lee's fame increased, so did the size of her baskets. This may have been at Abe's insistence if he believed he could ask more money for her larger works. But it's also possible Dat so la lee made the decision to create these enormous baskets on her own.

Abe so overpriced Dat so la lee's huge baskets that he found few buyers. At one point he spread the rumor she was going blind in an effort to raise the value of her work. His largest sale came in 1914 when a Pennsylvania industrialist bought one of her baskets for around $2,000. Abe also thought he might capitalize on Dat so la lee's fame by opening a museum to display her work. He approached the Pennsylvania investor again about buying more baskets to fund his venture, but the man refused and the museum never materialized.

The tours they took throughout the West and the accolades Dat so la lee received for her basketry encouraged the Cohns to look to the East for more customers. In 1919 they bundled up Dat so la lee and a young Indian girl and headed for the St. Louis Industrial Exposition.

Dat so la lee sat on a stage dressed in a simple, large-patterned dress with a scarf atop her head. She worked on a basket while Amy told her listeners that the Indian woman before them was a Washoe princess and the only person allowed to weave these particular designs. To hear Amy tell it, after a Washoe–Paiute war, the victorious Paiutes forbade Washoe women from weaving baskets.

But according to Amy, Dat so la lee secretly continued to weave, tossing the finished receptacles into the fire so she would not be discovered. By defying the Paiutes, said Amy, Dat so la lee became one of the few Washoe women to retain the knowledge of how to make the ancient designs. During these imaginative talks, Dat so la lee sat in the background, her head bowed, never uttering a word.

Amy died shortly after the group returned from St. Louis, and within a year Abe Cohn married again, much to the detriment of Dat so la lee and Charley. The new Mrs. Cohn saw no reason to keep the Washoe couple in such luxury, and their lifestyle declined under her care. No more pamphlets appeared lauding Dat so la lee's basketry. She did not weave as prolifically as when Amy was alive, and the baskets she created lacked the heart of her earlier designs.

Toward the end of her life, Dat so la lee suffered from what was then called dropsy (edema). She summoned a medicine man, but he was unable to help. She allowed a white doctor to treat her, to no avail. On December 6, 1925, Dat so la lee died in Carson City and is buried with her last unfinished *degikup* basket. She was around eighty years old.

Abe Cohn continued to peddle her baskets in his store but never realized the bonanza he had always anticipated from her artistry. He died in 1934 with more than half of Dat so la lee's baskets still languishing on his shelves. His second wife, seeing no value in the old bundles of willow branches, sold twenty of Dat so la lee's baskets to the state of Nevada for a mere $1,500. Today some of the old washerwoman's larger baskets are worth hundreds of thousands of dollars each.

Dr. Marvin Cohodas, the art expert who recognized Dat so la lee's missing baskets in 1998, credits her with "originating the popular curio style of Washoe fancy basket weaving, both because she introduced the finely stitched, two-color *degikup* and because she inaugurated individuality and innovation for others to follow."

Today Dat so la lee's baskets can be found in the Nevada State Museum in Carson City and the Nevada Historical Society in Reno, as well as in museums across the country. As reticent as she was to speak in public, her voice can still be heard through the artistry of her work.

HELEN JANE WISER STEWART
1854–1926

Las Vegas Legend

*T*he buckboard rattled across the barren desert, following trails first traipsed by nomadic Indian tribes. Mormon settlers and hopeful prospectors had also trod the barely visible path, seeking a better life and the fleeting promise of wealth hidden beneath desert asphalt. With one hand Helen Stewart clung to the unsteady wagon, wary of tumbling into the desert amid unforgiving cacti, hungry coyotes, and vengeful reptiles. With the other, she cushioned her unborn child. Her three youngsters bounced about in the back of the wagon among a handful of furnishings. As much as she hated this grueling ride, she dreaded her destination even more. The Stewart family had acquired a parcel of land in southern Nevada few deemed worthy of settlement, a place called Las Vegas Ranch.

Helen Stewart had not grown up amid the cacti and creatures of Nevada. Born in Springfield, Illinois, on April 16, 1854, the daughter of Hiram and Delia Wiser, Helen resembled "a tiny Dresden China piece," but proved through the years that even the most delicate work of art could be resilient in a harsh and unfor-giving setting. By the 1860s Hiram Wiser had settled his family in Sacramento County, California, and young Helen reveled in the social activities of a bustling, growing community.

At nineteen Helen met an Irish-born Scotsman, Archibald Stewart. Archie owned a successful freighting business near the mining community of Pioche, Nevada, hauling ore to nearby mills. Twenty years older than Helen, the distinguished-looking suitor wooed the petite young woman, and the couple married in Stock-ton, California, on April 6, 1873. The newlyweds immediately set out for Nevada and settled in Pony Springs, about 30 miles north of Pioche, where they leased land to start a cattle ranch.

Ranching in the 1800s consisted of long days and nights of hard work and little rest. Helen thrived on the physical demands but sorely missed the companionship of other women. The dis-tance between Pioche and Pony Springs was too far for casual social visits. When she discovered she was pregnant, the isolation of Pony Springs terrified her: She knew chances were slim another woman would be nearby to help when her time came.

Fortunately, William James Stewart arrived without much ado on March 9, 1874, but Helen was determined to be closer to aid and comfort before having another child. Archie agreed and moved his growing family into Pioche. On November 28, 1875, Hiram Richard was born, followed by Flora Eliza (Tiza) Jane on January 18, 1879.

Helen loved the little town of Pioche. It had passed its boom days of the 1860s and '70s, when prospectors dug up ore by the handfuls and men were killed on a whim. It was now a quiet com-munity and satisfied Helen's desire for close friends and neighbors.

In 1879 when Octavius Decatur Gass, a business acquain-tance of Archie's, could not pay the taxes on his ranch property, Archie loaned him $5,000 in gold bullion. Gass's 640 acres were

Helen Wiser Stewart

situated about 150 miles south of Pioche in a remote stretch of
land once part of Arizona Territory until it was transferred to the
state of Nevada in 1867. His ranch lay just a few miles from the
Colorado River, a rare and precious water source in the desert.
Mormon settlers first inhabited the area in 1855, leaving behind
an abundance of vineyards, fruit trees, and a handful of adobe
structures. Gass brought in cattle and added alfalfa fields to a cor-
nucopia of wheat, fruit, and vegetables nurtured by an underground stream.

When Gass could not repay Archie, he signed over the deed to
his ranch, plus an additional 320 acres. On May 2, 1881, Helen and
Archie became owners of 960 acres of prime land near a constant
water source, ideal for raising cattle, rearing children, and growing
crops. Archie decided his family should leave their comfortable
Pioche home and settle on their newly acquired Las Vegas Ranch.

Helen vehemently argued against leaving Pioche, where she
relied on the friendship of women who experienced the same joys
and sorrows, heartaches and heartbreaks. Moreover, she was pregnant again and dreaded another birth without a woman to assist
her. She had no desire to live in such a desolate area—the entire
population there totaled less than thirty souls.

Archie promised they would stay for only a year or so until he
found a buyer for the property. So in April 1882, Helen readied
her family for the road south.

The weeklong trek across miles of barren desert, attending to
the needs of her family, cooking and cleaning in the open, and
dealing with her pregnancy, left Helen more than a little disheart-
ened when she arrived at the run-down ranch. But she had chores
to do and a husband and children to look after.

By the time Evaline (Eva) La Vega was born on September 22,
1882, Helen had her household under control. Cattle thrived as

nearby streams replenished sun-dried grasses, peach and apple trees groaned under an abundance of fruit, grapevines bowed to the ground, alfalfa swayed in gentle breezes, and vegetables shot up toward the fiery sun.

Coming out of the desert after days of eating dust-covered meals, travelers relished the sight of Las Vegas Ranch. They stayed for days pampered by Helen. She encouraged them to linger as long as they wished, particularly the few women who showed up on her doorstep. As soon as she spotted wagons approaching, she stoked the fire, set the pot boiling, patted out fresh biscuits to pop in the oven, cleaned debris left by four spirited youngsters, and had the coffee perking by the time her guests hitched their horses and walked through the door.

As the ranch grew and profited, Helen worried about the amount of money kept in the house. Archie needed cash to pay the hired hands, and Helen often served as "banker" for prospectors concerned about entering lawless mining camps with large sums of cash. Archie traveled frequently to El Dorado Canyon near the Colorado River to sell beef and produce, and she never knew who might show up while he was gone. Busily scrubbing windows one day, she noticed a loose board above a window sash and pulled it off. As she peered into the crevice behind the board, she knew she had found her bank vault. Grabbing a bundle of money, she shoved it into the wall opening and replaced the board—her banking problems were solved.

On a July morning in 1884, Helen scooted her four rambunctious children out the door and set about her chores, aware she would soon have to slow down—she was pregnant again. As she cleaned the kitchen and readied the table for lunch, hired man Schyler Henry marched into the house, informed Helen that he was quitting, and demanded his wages. Archie was away, and since he always managed the men's pay, Helen informed Henry he would have to wait until Archie returned. What else was said between the two is unknown, but Henry may have threatened Helen before stomping out of the house and off the ranch.

A few days after Helen's run-in with Henry, Archie rode onto the ranch and brushed the dust from his pants, glad to be home. Helen prepared a hearty meal before telling him about Henry's tirade and untimely departure. It's doubtful that Henry's leaving bothered Archie, but when Helen related what else had transpired that day, Archie quietly left the house, rifle in hand. He knew he would find Henry at the Kiel Ranch a short distance down the road. The Kiels were known to shelter renegades and ne'er-do-wells, and they also harbored a deep hatred for the Stewarts stemming from an unresolved horse-rustling incident.

Who fired the shot that felled Archie that day remains a mystery. The bullets flew, and Archie was up against a whole stable of reprobates. When the dust settled, he lay dead with a bullet in his head.

When Helen received word of Archie's death, she suddenly realized she was now a widow with four—no, almost five—young children to rear alone.

In a letter to her attorney George Sawyer, Helen related the murder of Archie Stewart:

> As I got to the corner of the house I said Oh where is he Oh where is he and the Old Man Kiel and Hank Parish said here he is and lifting a blanket showed me the lifeless form of my husband. I knelt beside him took his hands placed my hand upon his heart and looked upon his face and saw a bullet hole about two inches above the temple and about one inch into the hair and looking more closely I saw where the Rifle had been placed directly under

the right ear and fired off burning most of the
whiskers off that side of his face to a crisp.

Helen used doors from the ranch to build a coffin for her
husband. In the searing Nevada heat, no time was lost burying the
dead. Archie was laid to rest the next day on a plot of land the
Stewart family would christen "Four Acres."

Now Helen was faced with running a household plus manag-
ing a busy ranch, all without the aid of another responsible soul.
"Helen Stewart was suddenly thrust into directing the operation of
the ranch," wrote historian Carrie Miller Townley, "a burden she
carried for the next twenty years."

On January 25, 1885, she gave birth to Archibald Stewart,
named for his dead father.

The children thrived on the rigors of ranch life. Helen tried to
teach them the morals and refinements of civility but felt she was
losing the battle to the wild desert and even wilder cowboys and
hired hands with whom her brood associated. In 1889 Oxford-
educated James Ross Megarrigle became part of her ranch family
as the children's teacher and her own mentor and trusted friend.
She loved listening to Megarrigle read his poetry, and the whole
family joined in when he played the fiddle or sang one of his dit-
ties. She considered him one of her better investments.

Helen's business acumen sharpened after her husband's death.
She eventually became the largest landowner in Lincoln County,
with more than 2,000 acres under her control. To help her father
start his own cattle ranch, she transferred a hundred head of her
cattle to his Nevada property. This alleviated her need for more
hired hands, yet she retained the right to sell her cattle whenever
she wished. She continued to deliver beef, hay, vegetables, and fruit
to settlements in El Dorado Canyon. When rumors circulated that

the railroad would soon lay tracks in the area, Helen bought as much land as she could afford, knowing property prices would skyrocket.

By now the Las Vegas Ranch had become the center of activity in sparsely populated southern Nevada. A polling precinct was established in 1890, with the ranch serving as the official voting site. Before 1893 mail was delivered to the area via circuitous and often perilous routes. Since Helen was already the unofficial messenger for passersby, her ranch hosted the first official Las Vegas post office, with Helen serving as postmistress until 1903.

Sons Will and Hiram handled many of the ranching and farming tasks—rounding up and branding cattle, harvesting crops, and selling livestock and produce to the highest bidders, all while keeping the ranch profitable. By 1896 both young men had married and were comfortably settled nearby.

With the ranch operating smoothly, Helen turned her attention to her three younger children. After teacher Megarrigle's death in 1894, their schooling deteriorated; she decided a California institution would provide more education than the wilds of Nevada. In 1897 she deposited Tiza, Eva, and Archie at a Los Angeles school. Young Archie particularly hated being away from the ranch, but he and his sisters returned each summer to revel in the freedom of the open range.

Home on vacation in July 1899, fourteen-year-old Archie rode off on his horse chasing wild mustangs, probably envisioning his prowess at taming one of the skittish beasts. Whether his horse lost its footing or Archie lost his grip, he fell headfirst onto the hard, rough ground. Helen buried her youngest child on the Four Acres property next to the father he'd never known.

Helen sold the Las Vegas Ranch in 1902 to the San Pedro, Los Angeles & Salt Lake Railroad for $55,000. She kept Four Acres, where the two Archies were buried.

When the railroad auctioned off lots that would eventually become the core of downtown Las Vegas, Helen bought 280 acres near her Four Acres property. From the front porch of her new home, she watched the building of a town that would become unlike any other in the world.

Of the hands who had worked on Las Vegas Ranch, Frank Stewart proved to be a gold nugget in disguise. Frank (no relation to Archie) had drifted and prospected around the West before wandering onto the ranch in 1886. After working his daily outside chores, Frank would volunteer to help Helen with the housework or sort mail in the post office, although he did like to sample the homemade wine and could often be found sitting under a shade tree tasting the latest batch of fermented grapes. Frank and Helen formed a close friendship and married on July 23, 1903, in Ventura, California.

Before the marriage, Helen asked Frank to sign a prenuptial agreement giving her sole control over her property. As Townley noted, ". . . Frank was never accorded the full status husbands enjoyed at the time. His wife remained the dominant partner in the marriage, retaining to a large degree the relationship established when Frank worked for her as a ranch hand."

Helen was delighted with the town growing around her. It bulged with businesses, railroad workers, and constant streams of new settlers. Houses and commercial establishments appeared almost overnight. One of Las Vegas's first streets was named for the pioneering Stewart family.

Society came to Las Vegas. Helen eagerly anticipated the arrival of newcomers after so many years living in the sparsely populated desert around the ranch. Most of her friends were farmers and ranchers whose social life centered on the dinner bell and a bunkhouse of hungry cowhands who knew nothing about social graces.

She certainly stood out among the townswomen when she entered the social fray. Receiving an invitation to tea from a newly arrived socialite, she marched into the woman's house, sat down in a rocking chair, and remained for the rest of the day. The hostess was aghast that Helen would ignore social etiquette that dictated a visit of short duration. She was quickly informed that western hospitality overruled societal norms and that Helen's home had always been open to any prospector, cowboy, farmer, or traveling family for as long as he wished to stay.

Along with being a part of Nevada history herself, Helen had a keen interest in the beginnings of the state and its Native people. Through the years, she acquired a vast array of Indian baskets, jewelry, and artifacts, eventually holding one of the most extensive collections in the state. When the southern division of the Nevada Historical Society was established in 1908, Helen became its first president.

In 1919 she expressed her desire that the state of Nevada become the caretakers of her collections after her death:

> I have many things I would like to have preserved for future benefit to my Home and State. My collection is not yet just as I would like it. I have spent much time and money in getting my collection as near perfect as I could. I have the reading of my Baskets and many Legends of the Indians which I wish to place in book form that they may be together a History of a people that has lived nearer to God and Nature than any race of people on the face of the earth.

Helen was instrumental in organizing one of Nevada's most influential women's organizations, the Mesquite Club. Representing the club, she lectured across the state touting Las Vegas's colorful beginnings and its Indian heritage.

Although now in her sixties, she became the first woman elected to the Clark County School Board and a founding member of the Society of Nevada Pioneers, formed in 1914. Governor Emmet Boyle appointed her a delegate to the Twelfth Annual Convention for the American Civic Association in Washington, DC, and in February 1916 Helen Stewart became one of the first women to sit on a Nevada jury. Sensitive to the plight of Indians who had lost their land, she donated acreage to establish the Las Vegas Paiute Indian Colony.

On September 1, 1918, Frank Stewart died. Once again, Helen buried one of her loved ones, only this time she did not lay Frank beside her first husband at Four Acres. Why Helen chose another location to bury him is unknown.

Shortly after Frank's death, Helen wrote to her daughter Tiza about the suffering she had watched him endure and the heartache with which she now lived. In that same letter, Helen expressed something of her own lifelong philosophy.

> But for me give me life as long as the Lord sees fit. To be born is life, to live, to enjoy, to suffer, and to die. But there are loved ones and loves in a way make us glad that life is ours, and pain and suffering for them a secret joy.

In 1924 Helen was diagnosed with cancer. Her days, weeks, and months revolved around trips to Los Angeles for sickening radium treatments, then back to Nevada to recuperate, all the while maintaining her busy social and business calendars. In a 1924 letter to Tiza, her sense of humor, despite her illness, remained strong. "Going to a Hospital makes quite a hole in ones Pocket

Book but that is better than being Dead for when you are Dead you are Dead a long time."

She started writing a book detailing her Indian artifacts. In 1925 her knowledge of Nevada history and her burgeoning collection of Nevada memorabilia prompted Governor James G. Scrugham to request she appear with some of her favorite pieces at the 1926 State Exposition in Reno. He had already appointed her to the Committee on Historical Research.

But Helen never made it to the exposition. Her death on March 6, 1926, marked the end of a spirit that had lit Las Vegas more than any future neon lights ever would. To honor the petite "First Lady of Las Vegas," businesses closed for the day; her funeral was the largest ever seen along the city's streets.

Although Helen wanted her vast collections of priceless Indian baskets and artifacts donated to the state of Nevada, many were sold to out-of-state buyers never to be seen again. But most people knew that the real treasure was the lady herself. Whether running one of the first successful ranches in southern Nevada, serving as postmistress, or contributing to the preservation of Nevada's past, Helen Stewart personified the determination and durability of Nevada's pioneering women.

There is no question that the desert was where her heart belonged. As she wrote to Tiza in 1924, "I would like to be in an Auto with a good driver and away out over the Desert. Just to ride and Ride away the hours til the night then home again."

Idah Meacham Strobridge

1855–1932

Sagebrush Scribe

*I*dah watched the scenery change from vivid green valleys and towering lush trees to stark desert as the train carried her from California to Nevada. She traveled alone, but not by choice, and only the altering vista brought a small smile to her lips. She ached for the comfort of home and craved to hear the trickling Humboldt River as it meandered through her property. What she left behind in Los Angeles haunted her thoughts; she occasionally felt the sting of tears running down her face. Now widowed and childless, she had decisions to make about the rest of her life, and she wanted to make them where the sun greeted her each day and the purple mountains cloaked her in their warmth. Home to Nevada, the only place that could heal her aching heart.

Idah Meacham Strobridge had brought her ailing husband and two children from Humboldt, Nevada, to Oakland, California, praying they would recover from the bone-chilling winter of 1888–1889 that had collapsed ranch house roofs burdened with accumulated snow, frozen cattle on their feet, and sent shivering prospectors to early graves. But the trip proved useless. Five-month-old Kenneth, and Samuel, her husband of only four years, died within weeks of their arrival. Only a few months passed before little Gerald joined them. Wasn't it enough she had lost her firstborn the day after his birth just three short years ago?

Even though snow still covered the stark landscape of her Nevada home, Idah's return to the ranch she and Samuel had built halfway between Winnemucca and Lovelock in Lassen Meadows filled her with hope. She knew that beneath the snow-crusted ground reposed great beauty.

Idah's roots lay in Moraga Valley, California, where she was born Laura Idah Meacham on June 9, 1855. When she was ten years old, her parents, George Washington Meacham and Phebe Craiger Meacham, moved to Humboldt to raise cattle after George had tried mining gold in California with little success. Nevada had become the thirty-sixth state in 1864 and offered a promising start to a new year.

Humboldt was located in one of the most isolated parts of the state, where an abundance of tall, lush grasses kept the family's cattle fat and salable. Idah relished the freedom the vast desert offered as it stretched beyond her imagination, a forecast of her future calling. "The other world of the desert she saw," said writer Anthony Amaral, "or, more adequately, felt as a place of awe and reverence for mind and body."

She loved to wander through the sparse sagebrush settings, enthralled with the high-desert landscape, towering mountains, and prickly plants. On hot afternoons she took her books and headed for her favorite reading spot, an old mine about a mile from her parents' home, where she lingered for hours among the relics of lost golden dreams. She encountered struggling prospectors, Paiute and Bannock Indians, Mexican and Chinese miners, and pioneers seeking a better life somewhere in the West. She listened for hours to the stories they told of wealth and wealth denied, ghosts and

Idah Meacham.
(enlarged photo. copy)

Idah Meacham Strobridge

mirages seen over the horizon. She learned how to pan for gold and seek out veins of silver.

Along with ranching, Idah's father built Humboldt House, a way station in the middle of the desert, serving hot meals and providing soft beds for weary travelers headed west and miners in search of elusive ores. When the Central Pacific Railroad crossed into Nevada in 1868, Humboldt House became a much-needed stop for citified easterners going on to California. Idah relished the mixture of voices that brought strange tales to her ears and new adventures to her dreams.

In 1878, at the age of twenty-three, Idah took all of these memories with her and returned to California to enroll in Mills Seminary (now Mills College) in Oakland to complete her education. Shortly after graduating in 1883, she met Samuel Hooker Strobridge. Although he was eight years her junior, their love flourished; the couple married in San Francisco on September 3, 1884.

Idah's parents gave the newlyweds a portion of their land to entice them back to Nevada. Idah needed no bribe to return to the desert. She ached for the purple mountains and golden desert floor, the rippling Humboldt River, and the assortment of people that populated the desert and regaled her with stories.

The house Idah and Samuel built on their 880 acres was no small cottage. Six bedrooms, two bathrooms, a parlor, sitting room, dining room, kitchen, sewing room, storeroom, dressing room, two pantries, three halls, and twelve closets meant there would be plenty of room for a growing family. Samuel ran running water into the house from a nearby well. Outside, a covered porch surrounded the house overlooking the Humboldt River, which ran through their property. They eventually added a workman's cottage, servant's house, barn, buggy house, water tank, icehouse, milk house, storehouse, blacksmith and carpenter shop, laundry, cowsheds, and chicken and pigeon houses. Fourteen miles of fencing had to be constantly monitored to keep wandering cattle, which sometimes numbered more than 8,000 head, corralled.

In December 1885 a son graced the Strobridge home—briefly. Baby Earl never gained the strength needed to start life on the isolated range; he died the day after his birth. He was one of scores of infants born to pioneer families who had little chance of surviving. Too many miles separated them from the nearest medical help. "Doctors were rare and hospitals nonexistent," according to historian Patricia Riley Dunlap. "In the face of extreme isolation and even abject deprivation, most first-generation pioneer women gritted their teeth and did what needed to be done. . . ." Health was a fragile commodity.

Idah and Samuel, determined to have a house full of rambunctious children, soon produced two more sons, Gerald and Kenneth. Idah looked forward to years of being regaled with dinner-table yarns of hunting, fishing, and cattle drives with the boys.

The fall of 1888 began mildly enough, but soon the winds whistled around the barn, seeming to call out to Idah and her family. Freezing rain, sleet, and snow pelted their ranch day after day, week after week. Idah kept the fire roaring, but that meant Samuel had to go out in the cold for more firewood no matter how hard the wind blustered or how deep the snow piled against their home.

Every day Samuel bundled up and headed out in a futile effort to save his herd, but the cattle froze where they stood with no hope of finding shelter. His treks through the freezing snow took a toll on him as well, and he was soon coughing up blood and weakening before Idah's eyes. She prepared hot, nourishing meals, but the fires were no longer bright and warm, for she now had to fetch the kindling herself—Samuel was too weak. Pneumonia settled in his chest, and soon he could no longer rise from the bed. Kenneth and Gerald began to show signs of the same fatal illness.

Remembering their useless efforts trying to save young Earl, Idah bundled up her family and headed for California, where doctors were more plentiful and the climate warm and inviting. She prayed for a miracle that might help her weakened husband and children, but it was not to be. Kenneth perished first. Before the end of the year, Samuel was gone. By winter's end, Gerald lay beside his father and brother.

Idah returned to her Humboldt home in 1890 with no husband, no children, and no cattle to keep her ranch going. But she was no quitter. Remembering the scraggly prospectors who had regaled her with their stories of riches, Idah tried her hand at gold mining. She discovered and worked several gold claims in the Humboldt Mountains, one of which was the elusive Lost Mine claim.

On July 13, 1895, forty-year-old Idah found herself the topic of a newspaper article in the *Mining and Scientific Press*, calling her the "New Woman" of Nevada:

> During the past four years persistent searches were made for the [Lost] mine, but each time were abandoned until this spring when a cultured woman of the new age appeared in the person of Mrs. Ida [*sic*] M. Strobridge, in company with a young man lately employed on her father's ranch near Humboldt. She is a most remarkably bright woman, and will climb a precipitous cliff where the average man would not dare to venture. In addition to mining she looks after the business of her father's cattle ranch, and is quite a sportswoman and would probably carry off first prize in a shooting tournament, as she brings down her game every time. She wears a handsome brown

denim costume, which she dons in climbing the very steep and rugged cliffs of the Humboldt Mountains. She has located five claims on the lode, laid out a new camp and named it after her father, "Meacham," and reorganized the district anew as the "Humboldt"; she has four men to work and is superintending operations herself. She has also located the water and springs flowing over her claims, which are nine miles east of the Central Pacific Railroad, at the Humboldt House. . . . Mrs. Strobridge is now engaged running a tunnel under the shaft where the vein is showing up finely, and if the present appearance is maintained the New Woman will in due time be reckoned a million-airess, and by her indomitable will and persever-ance. She is now sacking ores for shipment.

Unfortunately, the mine proved less profitable than predicted, and Idah had to seek other means of support. But she relished the time she spent in the rugged Humboldt Mountains among the juniper and piñon trees, prickly pear and hedgehog cacti, coyotes, bobcats, and rattlesnakes. She would later write:

> If you love the Desert, and live in it, and lie awake at night under its low-hanging stars, you know you are a part of the pulse-beat of the universe, and you feel the swing of the spheres through space. And you hear through the silence the voice of God speaking.

Her love of reading determined her next profession—she learned how to bind books. Turning her ranch house attic into the

Artemisia Bindery, Idah fumbled through her first attempts until she finally acquired a hand press, but, alas, she did not know how to use it. To the rescue came her father, who taught her the intricacies of running the press, even making some of her first tools. She later told a *Reno Evening Gazette* reporter, "The first thing you must have, if you want to learn bookbinding for a living, is a father."

Over the ensuing years, Idah received awards and accolades for the craftsmanship of her bindings. In 1908 at the California State Fair, she won a silver medal, and was awarded a gold medal at the Seattle Exposition in 1909. Then-editor of the *Los Angeles Times* Charles Fletcher Lummis was one of the first to recognize Idah's bindery talents: ". . . though this sagebrush artisan has been studying out this exigent trade by herself, off there in the wilderness, her work is emphatically worth while. A commercial-bound book looks cheap beside her staunch and honest and tasteful bindings. . . ."

During the time Idah was teaching herself the bookbinding trade, she began to write her impressions of the vast and lonely desert that stretched before her, and the strange, intriguing stories the old prospectors had repeated to her over the years.

Initially using the pseudonym *George W. Craiger*, a combination of her parents' names, Idah wrote in one of her first stories of her father's 1849 voyage aboard the ship *Orpheus* from New Jersey to the gold fields of California via the Isthmus of Panama. She wrote short stories and sketches and sent them to San Francisco and Los Angeles papers. The short-lived *Nevada Magazine* published some of her articles, as did *The Editor Magazine* in Franklin, Ohio.

Relying on the friendship she had already established with Charles Fletcher Lummis, Idah sent him some of her stories when he became editor of *The Land of Sunshine* publication. Lummis was delighted with her descriptive phrases that brought the desert to life, and he praised her work in a January 1901 editorial: "These stories and sketches are of the literary merit which inheres in directness, sincerity and impulse. It is not too much to call them well-written—but even more, they are well felt. They are earnest and honest work and of an excellent sympathy and strength." Idah had found her true vocation.

During the years Idah was establishing the Artemisia Bindery and beginning her writing career, the state of Nevada was in the throes of a depression. The population had actually diminished in the late 1800s, an unheard-of phenomenon among the growing western states. The lucrative Comstock Lode and other mining interests, which the state had heavily relied on to sustain its scattered population, dried up, and no other reliable means of industry had been established to sustain the economy. A lack of groundwater prevented productive ranching and agriculture. Even tourist sites such as the Grand Canyon or Yellowstone that attracted visitors to nearby states were nonexistent in Nevada. And as historian Walter Nugent lamented, "The railroad ran through it [Nevada], not to it."

Even though Nevada's economy picked up in 1900 with the discovery of ore in the Tonopah area, Idah felt it was time to move on. Her bindery work was growing rapidly, and if she could establish herself in a community of artists and writers, both the Artemisia Bindery and her writing might flourish. In the spring of 1901, she sold her ranch and headed for Los Angeles.

Acquiring at least $10,000 from the sale of her property, Idah bought a house in Los Angeles she named Sign of the Sagebrush, a remembrance of her Nevada roots. Her literary circle expanded; she counted Mary Austin, Margaret Collier Graham, Charles Wellard, Maynard Dixon, and her favorite publisher, Charles Fletcher Lummis, as her friends and neighbors. She reestablished the Artemisia Bindery and garnered awards for her bookbinding skills.

Idah's love of Nevada stayed with her as she wrote of the vast, peaceful desert that held so many memories for her. Her books overflowed with elaborate and explicit scenes of the desert, her treks up mountains searching for gold, and the tales she had heard from the assortment of characters she had encountered. True tales intertwined with adventures that stirred within her vivid imagination.

In her first book, *In Miners' Mirage-Land*, published by a Los Angeles company in 1904, Idah retold the old stories of wandering prospectors and pioneers winding their way through the Nevada desert. Mirages of ghosts, angels, and long-dead relatives encountered out on the desolate prairies permeate her tales, literal and imagined. "The mirage," said Idah, "is, in very truth, a part of the Desert itself—just as the sagebrush, and the coyote, and the little horned toads, and the sand-storms are part. To those who know Desert-land, the picture would be incomplete without them."

Who would not want to know what happens to "Old Man Berry" as she describes his trek across Nevada:

> Take up your map of the Western States. There, where the great Oregon lava flow laps over the State line of Nevada, in the north-western corner, lies the Black Rock country. Out there in that sweep of gray sand and sage-levels, and grim heights—the scaling of which—taxes the soul sorely, I found him—the typical prospector, "Old Man Berry," or "Uncle Berry," they called him. Over eighty years old he was, and for more than fifty years of his life led by the lure of a mirage.

When she was ready to publish her second book, *The Loom of the Desert*, in 1907, consisting of a dozen stories she had penned from 1899 to 1907, Idah knew she could produce a superior product within her own Artemisia Bindery. Dedicating to her parents "these stories of a land where we were pioneers," Idah's *Loom of the Desert* tales contain dark plots and unfinished pieces, leaving readers to uncover the endings within their own imaginations. As a *Los Angeles Herald* reviewer noted, "Those who love stories that quiver with life—that are intense in interest and action, will find the want satisfied in these tales."

Idah received praise across the country for her writings describing the Nevada wilderness. The *San Francisco Examiner* wrote, ". . . Mrs. Strobridge has penned these unusual stories that breathe of the desert and the desert people." In far-off Mobile, Alabama, the *Register* noted her writing was ". . . not the West of cowboys and Indians. . ., but the mysterious deserts with their tawny hills and their long gray stretches of alkali and fables of lost treasure . . . ." Years later, writer Anthony Amaral would christen her the "First Woman of Nevada Letters."

Idah's writing skills came to full force in *The Land of Purple Shadows*, published in 1909. Her protagonists are unforgettable characters that leave you turning the pages rapidly until the book lies exhausted at your feet. She had not forgotten her mining years in Nevada and the prospectors she encountered as she worked her claims hoping for that gleam of golden treasure: "Up and down the creek bed they move so noiselessly, working with pick and pan, that one can very easily fancy them but gray ghosts haunting the quiet cañons, even as the shadowy wraiths of the dead years linger about the unroofed walls and weed-grown trails."

One of her more poignant pieces describes a snowstorm, surely reminiscent of the winter of 1888 that wrested her family from her. In "The Quail's Cañon," albino mountains burst out of the frozen desert and loom over fallen trees, freezing nature's creatures as they sleep:

> There were nights when the storm roused itself to a fury that brought winds down from the heights roaring like wild beasts roaming through the cañon. The storm in its frenzy would beat against the rocks as though to rend them from their very foundations; and then would go shrieking over the ridge, and away. Morning would come, and the storm-fury would have spent itself; but not the snow. Always, and always it snowed. Each day dawned upon down-drifting flakes which fell upon a world of unearthly silence.

Idah issued her books in limited editions of about 1,000 copies. Those covered in ordinary wrappers sold for $6.75, while others adorned in leather bindings with hand-colored chapter headings were coveted at $10.00 each, quite expensive for the times. All were numbered and autographed by the author.

Although Idah told friends she had several more books in the works, her publishing career ended after her third book. She devoted the remainder of her years to genealogical research.

Idah never returned to Nevada, but she did create a retreat for herself in the wing of an old bathhouse in San Pedro, California, just west of Los Angeles, that she dubbed the "Wickieup." The fishermen in this tiny coastal town became her surrogate prospectors as they shared with her their meager fare and irresistible tales. In 1904 she told a *Los Angeles Examiner* reporter her reasons for creating this pseudo-desert oasis:

> It is not alone the open which attracts me and the

untrammeled natures of the people. It is the life utterly without pretense. I am not a city woman, neither do I like the country life which savors of the city. I despise the suburb. An existence wholly away from those conventional things hampered by man is what I long for. It is the life on the desert wholly apart from everything of pretense. I cannot give it up entirely and so I have furnished in fitting manner the "Wickieup," my substitute for the desert, down on the breakwater at San Pedro. The place is among the huts of fishermen and it is there that I go every Saturday night. I sit at the fishermen's tables and they sit at mine. . . .

On February 8, 1932, Idah Meacham Strobridge died in Los Angeles at the age of seventy-six; she is buried at Mountain View Cemetery in Oakland next to her husband and children. As one of Nevada's first women writers, she leaves a legacy of words coloring the mauve-tinged mountains and vast ranges of her beloved state to those who would willingly follow her into the Nevada desert.

Eliza Cook

1856–1947

Pills and Politics

*T*he dark, foreboding horse and buggy tore down the road, gritty dust devils ascending skyward attempting to avoid the careening carriage. Each passing house seemed to sigh in relief as the buggy lunged forward into the night. The driver, a woman who could barely reach the reins, held no fear of the rough terrain that lay before her.

Clad in black from head to toe, the woman walked into the house that was her destination and surveyed the surroundings. A figure lay motionless on a cot in the far corner. The other occupants of the house watched in silence as the woman leaned over the inert body and reached into her cavernous bag. She smiled at the bedridden soul, and then turned to the anxious family waiting in fearful expectation. Suddenly the shadow of death that had hovered so near the house for days seemed to evaporate into the dusty corners of the room. The doctor had arrived.

Eliza Cook traveled a road few women before her had dared. As one of the first physicians on the Nevada frontier, man or woman, she ministered to the sick and injured, the elderly and the newly

Eliza Cook

born, those who sought her out and those who declared they would never have a "doctress" come near them. Growing up during an era when most men who called themselves doctor had not attended medical school, when the healing art was more a guessing game than a scientific, lifesaving profession, Eliza discovered her calling for medicine at an early age.

One of five children born to John and Margaretta Gratrix Cook, Eliza made her appearance on February 5, 1856, in Salt Lake City, Utah. She later called her birth "an unappropriate blessing." Her father's belief in polygamy, plus his stinginess with money (he refused to buy shoes for his two daughters), encouraged Margaretta to leave her husband, taking Eliza and her sister, Rebecca, to Soda Springs, Idaho, then to White Pine County, Nevada. By 1870 the trio finally settled in Sheridan, Nevada, just south of present-day Carson City.

The threesome lived frugally. Margaretta took in laundry and sewed for the local townsfolk. Eliza once told a reporter the first Christmas gifts she remembered receiving were a cracker filled with raisins and a handmade wooden doll.

Few schools existed in Carson Valley when the abbreviated family arrived, and the two girls relied on their mother and a handful of borrowed books for their education. One of the books Eliza came across detailed home medical cures and remedies. This might have been a copy of William Buchan's book *Domestic Medicine*, which was first published in Scotland in 1769 and became popular in America about a hundred years later. Or she could have studied John C. Gunn's medical tome of the 1800s, *Domestic Medicine, or Poor Man's Friend*, in which he listed potions and poultices aimed particularly toward the western and southern states. Whatever she read, the book piqued her interest in medicine and she decided to pursue "doctoring" further.

Medicine of the 1800s offered scant cures for the sick and

injured. Dirty conditions, poor nutrition, and backbreaking work often made health a precious commodity. There were few proven remedies for the ill and injured. Folks usually found something that worked for one condition and used the same remedy repeatedly for whatever other ailments they encountered.

Women were expected to find solutions for their family's ills, often scouring their gardens and kitchens for cures. Eliza was fascinated with common household items that many believed resolved certain medical situations. She probably helped her mother with a common activity among frontier women—collecting raspberry, spearmint, and peppermint leaves, along with roots and bark, to alleviate ailments and illnesses. Mothers wrapped strips of raw bacon around their children's necks to soothe sore throats. Wood ashes applied to cuts helped curtail bleeding. Rhubarb bitters, catnip tea, carrot scrapings, and fresh snow were all thought to contain curative powers. In a pinch cactus fiber could be used to sew up a wound.

Religious and mystic beliefs also played roles in healing. Some sects refused to call a physician no matter how dire the situation. Others relied upon spirits of the dead to save a wretched soul. According to historian Ronald M. James, early Nevada pioneer Mary McNair Mathews claimed that "[w]hen one of her son's fingers was accidentally cut off, she placed it in a brandy jar, calling on a background in sympathetic magic, so that it would not hurt him in the future."

Shortly after reading the medical book she'd found, Eliza had the chance to use some of her elementary knowledge on her first patient. Dr. H. W. Smith hired her to nurse his ailing wife back to health. Mrs. Smith was suffering from puerperal fever, a condition usually originating in childbirth due to unsanitary conditions. The doctor had little in his black bag to ease his wife's suffering and became increasingly impressed with Eliza's care and concern for her patient. He offered her a job as his assistant and nurse even though she had no medical training.

Encouraged by Dr. Smith, Eliza read everything in his limited medical library. After about six months under his tutelage, Dr. Smith felt she was ready to enter one of the few medical schools that admitted women.

Over the years, women had repeatedly tried to enter all-male medical institutions, and the road had been rough and often unfriendly. The first woman to seek admission to a medical school was Elizabeth Blackwell in 1847. When she applied, she was informed the only way she could attend was if she dressed like a man. She refused. On her second attempt, she applied to Geneva Medical College in New York. School officials decided to let the all-male student body decide if she should be allowed to attend. After hearing her application, the men thought it was a joke and decided to go along with the prank by voting to admit her. To their great surprise, she readily accepted and completed her studies as a physician in 1849. The first women's medical school opened the following year.

Some male physicians felt the entrance of women into the medical community would threaten their practices economically. They argued that women were too frail and delicate to view the intimacies of the human body; they were too emotional to handle the horrors of surgery, the scourge of disease and human misery, the shame in examining a naked torso. Their hysterical nature and inferior intellect would prevent them from performing the more difficult tasks and would "harden women's hearts and leave them bereft of softness and empathy." These same practitioners, however, praised a woman's ability to take on strenuous nursing chores.

Of the seventy-five medical schools operating in the United States in the early 1880s, only a handful allowed women students. One of them, Cooper Medical College in San Francisco (now

Stanford University), had been admitting women for about five years when Eliza applied in 1882. She was accepted into its two-year program, considered all the education a doctor needed.

Eliza joined only a handful of women who were admitted into the prestigious medical community even though more than thirty years had passed since Elizabeth Blackwell had first walked into a classroom. Little had changed in the study of medicine during that time, but a few new procedures were now taught. Doctors had learned how to measure temperature, pulse, and blood pressure, even if they did not always know for what reason. Thermometers, tongue depressors, and stethoscopes appeared in medical bags alongside lances and probes. If the doctor appreciated the need for sterilization to ward off infection, she also toted along a copper pan in which to boil her instruments.

After graduating in 1884, Eliza set up practice in Sheridan at the home of her sister and brother-in-law, Rebecca and Hugh Park. She followed the routine of many women doctors, who returned to their hometowns where they had family and social connections, eliminating the burden of establishing businesses in locations where they were virtually unknown. Opening an office in her sister's home also gave Eliza, a single woman, a cloak of propriety when seeing patients.

The winter of 1889–1890 roared into Carson Valley like a stampede of Saturday-night cowboys headed for the closest saloon. With snowdrifts piled high across the plains, only the bravest dared to venture out. On a clear but bone-chilling day, a young boy skated as fast as he could across the frozen Carson River. Mr. Hickey had sent him on a mission—Mrs. Hickey was ready to have her baby and needed the doctor quick.

Hugh Park hitched up the horses and sleigh to take Eliza on the treacherous 3-mile ride. But the snow was too deep; the horses would never make it to the Hickey place. Ingenuity being an absolute necessity in the early West, Park and three of his neighbors crafted a sleigh from old snowshoes, settled Eliza and her black bag in the back, strapped themselves to the front of the makeshift sleigh, and set off across the valley.

When Mr. Hickey, who was probably pacing outside the house waiting for the doctor to arrive, saw the human-drawn sleigh plowing through the heavy snow, he greeted the men with a wee bit of Irish whiskey. Eliza, a temperance advocate since early childhood, chastised the men before disappearing into the house to attend to Mrs. Hickey. Little James Hickey arrived several hours later. Eliza and her four-man team strapped themselves into their makeshift sled and headed out across the drifting snow for the long ride home.

Aware she must continue her studies if she was to compete with the medical men of Nevada, Eliza attended classes at the Women's Medical College of Philadelphia in 1890, one of a handful of female medical schools that had cropped up as more women sought careers in medicine. The following summer she pursued graduate work at the Post Graduate Medical College in New York.

Returning to Nevada in 1891, she at first opened an office in the Golden Eagle Hotel in Reno, but stayed only six months before returning to her roots in Sheridan. There Eliza tended to a community of Nevada women and men who brought her their broken bones, illnesses without names or cures, scalded hands from open fires and boiling water, bites from snakes, scorpions, and spiders. She made her own splints and created some of her own concoctions for treatment of these ills as well as ordering other remedies through the mail. Each dose of medicine was carefully wrapped in a sterilized piece of tissue paper.

Many of her patients were pregnant women, who welcomed the compassionate caring of another female during childbirth.

Eliza understood that a homestead in early Nevada relied on a mother's hand to keep food on the table, livestock fed, and children clothed and educated while the man of the house left each day to work in the mines or plow the fields. If a new mother was unable to leave the birthing bed and tend her household, everyone suffered.

As Dr. Cook's reputation grew, women knew a call to her meant the family would receive care beyond the birthing of a newborn. Eliza arrived to bring a new life into the world and care for the mother, but for days afterward she'd return to the remote farmhouse or ranch to care for the family—washing clothes, cleaning dishes, cooking, and performing general housework.

By the end of the nineteenth century, more than 7,000 women were practicing medicine in the United States, although the American Medical Association did not acknowledge them until 1915. Women doctors were still a rarity in Nevada as late as 1918 when a census listed only eight licensed female doctors, two of them retired and only one who had been practicing longer than Eliza.

For many years Eliza, along with many others, believed she was the first woman to practice medicine in Nevada, but a good many doctresses had in fact preceded her. Since physicians were not licensed in the state until 1899, and Eliza was the first woman to receive a state-issued medical license, the assumption remained unquestioned for some time.

There was another side to Eliza: She abhorred the evils of alcohol. Even as a child, she was repelled by the use of liquor, joining a youth temperance group, the Band of Hope, when she was fourteen years old. When the women of Carson Valley formed a local chapter of the Women's Christian Temperance Union, she became actively involved and served as president from 1896 until 1901. She often lectured on the evils of drink and admitted she "made myself very objectionable at times, I've no doubt." No wonder she was appalled when Mr. Hickey brought out the whiskey before she delivered his son.

At the same time she was involved with the Band of Hope, young Eliza read a passage in the Bible that disturbed her. Genesis 3 says in part, ". . . thy desire shall be to thy husband and he shall rule over thee." In an interview with the *Nevada State Journal* in 1941, Eliza remembered the words she had read many years before. "That man should rule over woman was to my mind most unjust," she said. "I protested to my mother and she told me the husband's rule was right only when it was a righteous rule." Margaretta had already experienced the unrighteous rule of her own husband. "That silenced my tongue for a time, but not my mental protest." Equality for women was another cause Eliza embraced.

As she did with everything she challenged, Eliza took on the women's suffrage movement with a vengeance. A letter she wrote to the *Reno Evening Gazette* in 1894 outlined her views on a woman's right to vote, succinctly laying out her platform. She argued she would never feel "a citizen of these United States, . . . until I have the rights and privileges of the masculine citizen."

She did not mince words in her tirade against the world's assumption that man was a more intelligent and worldly person than his female counterpart:

> . . . man cannot fill woman's place in the economy of nature nor in social economy. How then can he fill her place in the political economy of the nation?

> . . . I believe in the fullest development of every human being, and believe that this can never come except through activity of all the faculties. I believe

the responsibility of citizenship will arouse the dormant powers of some of our women.

. . . I believe a woman fully as capable of assisting in the government of the nation as the government of the home, and I have observed that the greater portion of the latter is left to her.

. . . [I]f to vote is the evidence of a man's freedom and citizenship, the absence of that right shows that woman is neither free nor a citizen.

In October 1895 women from across Nevada gathered at McKissick's Opera House in Reno to establish the Nevada Women's Equal Suffrage League. Eliza was elected one of the first vice presidents and later became president of the Douglas County Equal Suffrage League. Diligent in her quest for a woman's right to vote, she often lectured to groups in the evenings after long days tending to the physical needs of the community.

In 1896 Eliza published a missal on the rights of women. Titled *The Woman Yet to Come*, it outlined the duties of a woman who has equal status. While she would be far from perfect, tomorrow's woman had the duty to "do more and better work than we do because [she will be] better prepared. . . . Surely, she who cleans is as worthy as they who make unclean!"

The text continued, "As a citizen, our coming woman will be as active as such a woman should be, and will aid by voice and vote in establishing the right. She will not be a political cipher, and consequently will take an active, intelligent part in all governmental affairs."

Unlike many of her suffrage counterparts, Eliza lived long enough to see the women's rights bill pass in the state of Nevada in 1914. In 1920 it became the Nineteenth Amendment to the U.S. Constitution.

By 1901 Eliza needed a break from the rigors of running a medical practice, as well as working for women's suffrage and fighting a losing battle for temperance. She talked a friend into spending a year traveling with her to the Holy Land, Greece, Egypt, the British Isles, and Europe. When she returned, she lectured on her travels, much to the delight of her Carson Valley neighbors, some of whom had never ventured more than a few miles beyond their own front doors.

In 1911 Eliza built a home in Mottsville, Nevada, that became her sanctuary from the trials of a medical practice and her work with the suffrage movement. She relished the time she spent working in her garden and abundant apple orchard. On a 3-foot woodstove, she filled her house with the aroma of freshly baked apple pies, one of which usually accompanied her when she set out to deliver a new baby. She dispensed dozens of homemade cookies to her younger patients, and continued to treat the ills of the community until 1921 when, at the age of sixty-five, she decided she had practiced long enough.

Although she no longer tended to the physical needs of her patients, for the next twenty years she continued to treat their hearts by crocheting small outfits for almost every newborn in Carson Valley. Their stomachs she soothed by making sure every child she encountered received a cookie hot from her tiny oven, or a crisp, shiny apple from her orchard.

Dr. Eliza Cook died in her sleep at her home in Mottsville on October 2, 1947. Beside her lay a handwritten document, "Outline of My Life," in which she briefly told of her early childhood, her medical practice, and her work with the suffrage and temperance movements. She lived ninety-one years and witnessed a vast number of changes both in the medical field and in women's rights. She was representative of the emerging woman of the twentieth century, capable of performing any task she set out to do.

DAUGHTERS
OF CHARITY
1864–1897

Angels on the Comstock

*T*he road to heaven is filled with challenges and demands. The road to St. Mary's in the Mountains Catholic Church in Virginia City, Nevada, resembles the pathway to a more perilous destination. Rocky inclines and unpredictable winds cause even the most devout parishioners to utter words of discouragement. Washoe zephyrs, gales that unpredictably roar down nearby mountains, gleefully dispatch even the most tightly tied bonnets. Worshipers ascend to the church with heads bowed, not in reverence but to avoid tumbling down the precipice upon which the majestic edifice stands. Amid this treacherous setting, the Daughters of Charity challenged the incline to the church on a daily basis and delighted in the blustery winds that promised to carry them nearer to God.

On October 7, 1864, just weeks before Nevada became the thirty-sixth state of the Union, Sisters Frederica McGrath, Xavier Schauer, and Mary Elizabeth Russell caught the Pioneer Stage out of San Francisco heading for Virginia City, Nevada. Virginia City was part of the great Comstock Lode that had emerged just five short years before when gold and silver were discovered in the town's surrounding hills. With a population consisting of thousands of miners, gamblers, and cowboys, most living in tents and all bent on finding a fortune and having a good time, the noisy town never lacked for excitement. Trains arrived and departed continuously, dynamite blasted from the mines to shake the unstable ground beneath the city's streets, and all day long the deafening roar of stamp mills echoed off the hillsides. Gunfights made the streets perilous and unfit for respectable women and innocent children. Schools were almost nonexistent. Murder, illness, disease, and abandonment left dozens of children destitute and homeless, begging for handouts at saloon doors, gambling halls, and houses of ill repute.

The arrival of the Daughters of Charity in Virginia City began a new era in education and community service on the Comstock. Founded by Vincent de Paul and Louise de Marillac in Paris, France, in 1633, the Daughters of Charity are dedicated to serving the "poorest of the poor." In 1809 Elizabeth Ann Seton initiated the Sisters of Charity of St. Joseph in Emmitsburg, Maryland, and in 1850 the two religious organizations merged into a unified, worldwide affiliation. After that time the terms *Daughters* and *Sisters* of Charity were used interchangeably.

Breaking with traditional cloistered orders that stayed within the confines of their nunneries, the Daughters of Charity preferred going out among the people to offer comfort and care. Thirty-nine-year-old Sister Frederica McGrath was well prepared to handle the physical needs as well as the spiritual and educational demands of Virginia City's citizens.

Alice Eliza McGrath was ten years old in 1835 when she and her parents, Alice English and John McGrath, arrived in Philadelphia, Pennsylvania, from the village of Doon in County Tipperary, Ireland. Eight more years elapsed before she took her vows with the community of Mother Seton's Sisters of Charity in Emmitsburg,

No child was ever turned away from the Daughters of Charity School and Orphanage. This sketch, drawn by artist and former Daughter of Charity Georgia Hedrick, personifies the care and concern the Daughters provided while also depicting the fun-loving, carefree side they displayed with their small charges.

where she was given the name Frederica. After spending several years teaching in Catholic schools along the East Coast, she was called to serve in San Francisco.

As one student later remembered, Sister Frederica was known to be "strict and firm in the class-room, but on the play-ground she became a child with the children, joining in our sports, teaching us all kinds of new games, and entering heart and soul into our amusement." Sister Frederica eventually became principal of St. Vincent's Boys' School in San Francisco.

When Father Patrick Manogue, one of the most important religious men in Virginia City, saw the necessity for a school in the rough and rowdy town, he requested the Daughters of Charity send a delegation from San Francisco to educate his young flock. Under the leadership of Sister Frederica, Sisters Xavier and Mary Elizabeth were chosen to go into the tempestuous territory of the Comstock.

Within days of their arrival, the sisters opened the doors of St. Mary's School. According to the *Virginia Daily Union*, fifty "female children attended school the first day and, no doubt, the number will be largely increased in a short time." Some children boarded with the sisters; initially everyone lived together in the 60-by-35-foot basement of St. Mary's in the Mountains Church. For heat, they relied on a potbellied stove that huffed out billows of smoke but never quite spewed enough warmth to take the chill off the tiny cubicle. The sisters' first objective was to find a suitable building for their school.

In addition to establishing a school, the Daughters were soon taking in orphans, for these young Comstock "throwaways" had nowhere else to go. Never banishing any child from their doorway, the sisters treated all their charges equally. When Sister Frederica realized many of the orphans had never been taught the simplest of games, however, she took them to the surrounding hilltops and showed them how to fly kites. Before long, children were running alongside kite-flying sisters up and down the hills of the ramshackle town, their laughter penetrating into the deepest mine shafts. The sisters didn't just watch their young charges play ball, either, but stood at the plate hoping for a home run as tiny outstretched hands reached for a fly ball.

With the overwhelming need to obtain a suitable facility, the Daughters organized what would be the first of many fund-raising fairs. Booths offered homemade foodstuffs and games of chance. A variety of races challenged the young and not so young. As the day turned to evening, and after the Daughters had retired for the night, local musicians played while dancers waltzed and jigged. Over the years some of these events garnered as much as $16,000 during weeklong festivities. The editor of the *Gold Hill Daily News* attended the first event in December 1864, claiming he left "minus four bits" after only ten minutes.

In January 1865 Sister Frederica wrote to Father Burlando, the sisters' spiritual director, reporting there were "in the house twenty in all, three of whom are orphans—four I might say worse than orphans for their parents are separated; the remaining ones boarders, paying what they can."

Meals at St. Mary's School and Orphanage, as it became known, provided generous portions but were not overly diverse.

"Is breakfast ready, Sister?"

"Sit down, child, and I'll fix you a big plate of corned beef."

"Whatcha cooking for lunch, Sister?"

"Corned beef and cabbage—yummy!"

"Sister, what are we having for dinner?"

"Tonight, we're having a rare treat, cabbage and corned beef."

Citizen donations filled the larder, with beef a daily staple. For a long time one local miner secretly deposited a pitcher of milk on the orphanage doorstep every morning.

For a fee of $25 a month, the students studied from a curriculum of more than twenty subjects ranging from the three R's to the arts and sciences. Yet if a mining accident felled a family's breadwinner, the children were allowed to remain without charge. Everyone helped with daily chores, including the arduous task of baking eighty loaves of bread three times a week to feed the ever-hungry youngsters. With many items in short supply, children usually brought their own sets of silverware from home.

As the student population increased and funds were stretched to unmanageable limits, Sister Frederica incorporated the school and orphanage, which allowed the Daughters to request funds from the state legislature. In 1867 they began receiving $2,500 annually from the legislature to maintain their facility. Controversy surrounded the decision to support the Catholic-operated complex even though religion was never an issue when a child needed a place to stay. There was also dissension as to whether the sisters should admit nonwhite children. According to historian Ann Butler, some officials wanted only white children to be housed at the state-supported facility, and the *Gold Hill Daily News* agreed. The *Territorial Enterprise*, however, favored continuing the funding only if all Nevada children, regardless of race, were accommodated.

While these rumblings continued along legislative hallways, the Daughters of Charity tended to the ills of the rest of the town. They were a calming force whether the problem involved a mining accident or fatality, family illness or barroom brawl. Usually the first to arrive when a mine tunnel collapsed, the Daughters tended to broken bones and broken hearts, and were always on hand to offer a warm meal to anyone in need of a handout. According to Butler, they plied jail inmates with "food for the body and soul." Their visits to comfort the ill at the Storey County Hospital, about 7 miles from town, became so frequent they were once listed, erroneously, as part of the hospital staff. The county facility had the reputation as a place where death was inevitable. Sometimes paying a whole day's wages to be admitted to the hospital, miners were lucky if they ever saw a doctor again.

One night a heavy pounding on the sisters' door found a distraught Irishman demanding to see Sister Frederica. A young girl was dying at the county hospital, he said, and begging for a priest, but the hospital superintendent had refused her request. Sister Frederica wasted no time gathering a priest and another sister, grabbed a carriage, and headed for the hospital. (No Daughter traveled with a man, even a priest, without another sister present for fear of gossip.) Leaving the priest to confront the disgruntled superintendent, the two sisters comforted the dying girl, who again asked for a priest. Sister Frederica found the superintendent locked in eye-to-eye combat with the priest, and, as the young sister who accompanied her later recalled, Sister Frederica "in her own mild way, at once gained her point." The priest was "conducted without delay to the poor girl who had the happiness of receiving the Last Sacraments."

Each day began at 4:00 A.M. for the Daughters. Getting dressed was probably the longest chore they performed. The Holy Habit was not at all suitable for Virginia City's steamy summer climate and windy winter days. "When I wore it," said former sister Georgia Hedrick, "it felt like a ton, but I got used to it. I could even run with it, and roller skate and play ball. In reality it weighed an extra 15 pounds."

The heavy, multilayered outfit was hand sewn, and with only three habits allotted each sister during her lifetime, they were put together with a particularly fine seam. First each sister donned a white cotton chemise, then a corset and petticoat. Next, two enormous pockets, hanging to the knees, were tied over the petticoat. She then put on a blue wool skirt. A woolen jacket, or chemisette, was hooked to the skirt. All these garments were topped with a matching apron consisting of one large pocket on the side. Sister Frederica usually managed to find a piece of candy deep within at least one of these pockets to soothe a small, distraught soul.

The sister's chaplet, or rosary, hung down the front of her skirt. In later years, as her eyesight faded, Sister Frederica removed the chaplet from her waist and hung it around her neck so she could easily touch it whenever she wished.

A large, wide, heavily starched white collar, resembling a knight's protective breastplate, was pinned securely around the neck and hung, unattached, down the front of the costume. This collar, however, simply would not stay down on windy days when Washoe zephyrs spilled out of the mountains. As strong breezes whooshed up and under the flapping collars, the sisters found it impossible to keep track of a flying kite or accurately hit a baseball.

All these articles of clothing were hot and heavy, but they were nothing compared to what sat on a sister's head. The cornette was a stiffly starched, extremely uncomfortable, 3-foot wide, white-winged hat shaped like an overgrown dove. In fact, Paiute Indians, upon seeing the sisters for the first time, called them "the great white birds that prayed." According to Hedrick:

> The wind was something the Sisters in Virginia City talked about in their letters—Washoe zephyrs they called them—sweeping down the hillside in full force and sudden as a summer rain shower. One lived in fear that the headpiece would be blown off. That cornette was like living in a tunnel . . . You could hear your own voice echo in it and you could not see left nor right, just straight ahead. I remember when we changed the Habit to a veil, it felt like coming out of a cave. . . .

After donning all this garb, the sisters climbed the hill to St. Mary's in the Mountains Church for morning services, returned to the school to prepare breakfast for the children, back up the hill to the church for meditation, then down the hill to boil water for the laundry and start baking. Up the hills, down the hills. According to one of the sisters, but also credited to *Territorial Enterprise* reporter Mark Twain, getting around Virginia City was like living on the side of a roof.

By 1870, with discussions still raging over how St. Mary's School should be run, Sister Frederica withdrew her request for state funds, chastising the legislature for its "heartless indifference for parentless children." By then the state had started its own orphanage in Carson City and had no interest in continuing its financial relationship with the Daughters of Charity. In a letter to the *Territorial Enterprise*, Sister Frederica berated the legislature for harboring anti-Catholic sentiment and jeopardizing the welfare of Virginia City's orphans. "We have no salary or wages; we have consecrated our life, our time, our attention, our care and all that this world could afford us, to help the distressed, the afflicted and especially the poor orphan." Even without state funds, the sisters continued to take in Nevada's lost children.

In 1875 the Daughters of Charity determined that Virginia City needed a hospital of its own. Estimating it would cost around $40,000 to build, they sought the support of the town's more affluent citizens, such as Mary Louise Mackay, wife of Comstock millionaire John MacKay. Mary Louise had once taught at St. Mary's School, and she never forgot the compassion of the sisters at a time when she was destitute. Now with an abundance of wealth, she gave the sisters six acres of land on which to build their new hospital. While Sister Frederica continued to run the school and orphanage, Sister Ann Sebastian arrived to manage the hospital staff. On March 15, 1876, the first patient was admitted to St.

Mary Louise Hospital, named for its generous benefactor.

The four-story brick hospital accommodated up to seventy patients. Five public wards and twelve private rooms enjoyed the warmth of steam heating provided by donated coal and wood. Bathrooms on every floor even included showers, and the operating room was equipped with both hot and cold water. A chapel window opened onto one of the wards, allowing bedridden patients to participate in services. Eventually balconies were added, allowing patients to recover in Virginia City's almost constant sunshine.

Gardens of flowers, fruit trees, and vegetables supplied patients with brilliant arrays of color along with healthy meals. For payment of $1.00 a month, miners and their families now had a hospital from which they could walk away, patched up and healthy, ready to return to work.

One newspaper article describing the facility claimed it was "so well ventilated that not the slightest odor, characteristic of hospitals in general, can be detected in any portion of the building."

According to historian Ronald M. James, the hospital "stands as a testimony to the humility and hard work of the Daughters of Charity. Affording themselves few comforts, those who worked in the facility were promised long hours filled with unending tasks through which to express their devotion to God."

The hospital, school, and orphanage were not the only facilities flourishing under the care of the Daughters of Charity. Standing on its rocky, windswept hillside, St. Mary's in the Mountain Church prospered under their tender mercies. Their compassion was never needed more than when, on a dry and windy day, a lantern tipped over at "Crazy Kate" Shea's boardinghouse. The Great Fire of October 1875 took only a few hours to sweep across the town, destroying over thirty-three city blocks including the entire business district. Buildings crumbled while families fled with what they could carry. Nothing seemed to tame the fire's fury, and St. Mary's in the Mountains Church stood in its path.

When the winds quieted and snow began falling that night, St. Mary's Church lay in eerie silence, its roof and wooden frame smoldering in ashes. The sturdy brick walls, however, remained intact against the ash-gray sky. The town's citizens, regardless of religion, and with John and Mary Louise Mackay the driving force, donated their time and money to rebuild the church that many considered the cornerstone of Virginia City.

In the mid-1880s, St. Mary's School housed about 100 students with an additional 200 attending classes during the day. Sister Frederica, by then in her sixties, had been superioress since the school's inception in 1864. The Motherhouse in Emmitsburg, Maryland, determined she had served enough time in rowdy Virginia City. They sent Sister Baptista Lynch to replace her as administrator, and in 1886 Sister Frederica left the Comstock. She spent her remaining years teaching in California schools, and died in San Francisco on April 18, 1913, at age eighty-eight.

Her obituary notice in the *San Francisco Monitor* lauded her as the "Angel of the Camps . . . whose life was one of the last links that bound us to the early days of adventure and excitement; who half a century ago, was the angel of charity in the wildest and richest mining camp of the world—the historic Comstock." She is remembered today as the most beloved of the "great white birds that prayed."

By 1897 the mining industry had fallen on hard times, and only a marginal population kept Virginia City from turning into a ghost town. A handful of sisters remained on the Comstock ministering to the needs of the community. Finding it exceedingly difficult to raise the necessary funds to support the hospital and school, the Daughters petitioned the Motherhouse to relieve them of their duties. Sister Ann Sebastian probably wrote the last entry in the hospital's logbook: "The Sisters of Charity left for good, Sep 7, 1897." For thirty-three years more than fifty Daughters of Charity had served on the Comstock; two are buried there. Their devotion to serving the "poorest of the poor" continues worldwide today.

Spirits, myths, and ghost stories are an integral part of Virginia City's lore, and the Daughters of Charity are the subjects of several legendary yarns. Some say they have seen horse-drawn hearses waiting outside St. Mary Louise Hospital, now St. Mary's Art Center, to collect the dead, steam rising from the impatient horses as they snort in the night air. A white nun is said to float along the hallways tucking blankets around sleeping art students. Georgia Hedrick may have solved some of the apparition sightings when she discovered that five sightseeing Daughters visited the old hospital in the late 1950s before it became an art school. Finding the building boarded up, they pried open a window and climbed inside. As they explored the rooms and wandered upstairs, perhaps an old-timer, returning from an afternoon at a local saloon, saw the sisters in the dirty windows and imagined they were nuns from the past.

The Daughters of Charity will long be remembered in Virginia City as a gentle force that brought education along with fun and laughter to the town's children while tending to the bodies and souls of the rest of the town. They did "more than staff a school and a hospital," said Ann Butler. "They had made a home and built personal relationships in the little mountain town. Their departure created a permanent void in the social institutions of Virginia City, as well as in the emotions of those comforted by the presence of the sisters with the blue gowns and white cornettes."

JOSEPHINE REED PEARL

1873–1962

Last of the Calico Prospectors

*E*very day Josie Pearl rose before dawn, ate and occasionally bathed, fed the chickens, surveyed the landscape surrounding her cluttered shack, stuffed a few pieces of bread or maybe last night's leftovers in a pack, slung a pickax over her shoulder, and headed out across the stark Nevada desert to find her fortune. She might walk if she was going a short distance, or climb into her rickety truck and head toward a distant spot that might yield a glimmer of gold or silver. Shoving her pack beneath a large boulder offering the only shade for miles, she would raise the pickax above her head and begin another day.

The sun burned into her leathery skin. Sweat seeped through her tattered calico dress, making it appear darker, thus giving the garment an artificial look of newness. She pounded relentlessly on unyielding rock, wary of sharp slivers that flew in every direction and would certainly penetrate her ill-fitting, dirt-encrusted boots. As she raised the pickax to a particularly large boulder, a cascade of brilliance emanated from her hands and wrists. Thousands of dollars' worth of diamonds blazed against the heat-searing sun.

Lowering the ax to examine what she extracted from the

stubborn rock, she ran her coarse hands across the razor-sharp shards, stopping momentarily to admire her jewels. More than sixty years of backbreaking work in Nevada's gold and silver fields was the price she had paid to attain these precious gems. She quickly dismissed the glittering diamonds and took up her pickax again, determined to convince the stubborn boulder to yield its bounty. It was the thrill of the hunt rather than the prize that kept her looking for untenable wealth.

Josie Pearl mined her way across Nevada from the early 1900s until her death in 1962. She fought off claim jumpers and corrupt businessmen hell-bent on stealing her hard-earned strikes. She is one of the last known women to make a living in the stark, majestic Black Rock Desert in northern Nevada. And in the end, the only thing she had left to show for her toil and trouble was a handful of diamonds that sparkled in the sun.

Working hard was a way of life for Josie. Born in Evening Shade, Arkansas, on December 19, 1873, she was among the twelve children born of John Everett and Priscilla Adair Reed. As the family grew, so did the need to find richer, more plentiful farmland. Two years after Josie's birth, they headed to Lexington, Tennessee, near the Natchez Trace, and several years later relocated to Los Cerrites, New Mexico. By the time Josie was eight years old, they had finally settled in Colorado on a ranch in the San Luis Valley.

The Reeds had few possessions. Their Colorado home was built of sun-dried adobe bricks with a door frame constructed from cottonwood tree branches. A piece of cloth covered the doorway. Small panes of glass embedded in the interior mud-brick walls sufficed for windows but lacked openings for ventilation. When John Reed was able to snare a wild rabbit, they had meat for dinner. More often, meals consisted of root vegetables and wild herbs.

As a youngster, Josie learned the value of working hard. With

Josephine "Josie" Pearl, June 1951

a wire-toothed brush called a card, she smoothed out woolen fibers before spinning them into fabric for the family's clothing. She hired herself out to neighbors cleaning houses and removing unwanted sagebrush from fields. After she landed a job sweeping the schoolhouse for 25 cents a week, she purchased a pair of shoes even though they were too small for her. Only wearing them on special occasions, she removed them immediately afterward, much to the relief of her cramped toes.

When Josie's father decided to try his luck mining in the Tres Piedras, New Mexico, area, twelve-year-old Josie begged to go as his cook. With eleven other children at home, her absence meant one less mouth to feed.

Josie loved the freedom she was allowed in Tres Piedras. Her cooking chores took up only a portion of her day; then she was free to roam. The rocks she found near the mines intrigued her, and she soon learned to identify those containing flecks of gold. Although this was her first experience with "gold fever," what she really caught was tick fever, forcing her to return to her mother in Colorado to recover.

Josie had listened well to the miners at Tres Piedras when they argued the best methods of locating gold veins and promising outcrops. By the time she was thirteen years old, she could distinguish between fool's gold (iron pyrite) and the real thing, and staked her first claim, the Molly S. Since she was underage, her father filed the claim for her and almost immediately received an offer of $5,000 for it. Most of the money went to pay the family's debts.

With a little of her Molly S. money, Josie decided to further the culinary career she'd started in Tres Piedras by enrolling in Peck's Training School in Denver, a cooking institution. In 1887, at the age of fourteen, she headed out alone for the gaslights of the big city.

Denver was a revelation to the unsophisticated farm girl, but she learned her craft well and was soon working as a mining camp cook in Leadville. In 1890 she moved to Creede, Colorado, and cooked at the Zang Hotel. Josie's biographer, Alma Schulmerich, described Creede as "the smelliest place she [Josie] had ever set foot in, running the gamut from manure, unclean bodies, tobacco, liquor, and the cheap perfume which emanated from the bawdy houses and saloons located every couple of doors!" When the tall, attractive young blonde walked to work along Creede's crowded streets, she garnered her share of suitors, and one in particular caught her eye.

Six-foot-tall mining engineer Lane Pearl had received his education at Leland Stanford University in his home state of California. Lane and Josie made an odd couple with his academic background and her all-but-nonexistent schooling, but the pair thrived in each other's company and married in 1903. Josie was working as a nurse at a hospital at the time and prospecting every spare moment. Lane managed the Happy Thought Mine near Creede.

The couple went where there was work for both of them, following ore strikes around the West. They lived for a while in California, then moved to Reno where Josie nursed at Whittaker Hospital. When Goldfield, Nevada, experienced a flush of good fortune around 1904, the Pearls took off again. Waitressing at the Palm Grill in town, Josie described the restaurant as "elegant," a term she would continue to use for many of the places and people she came to know. Married women were not allowed to work at the Palm Grill, so the Pearls told no one of their union. When Lane came in to eat, he sat at Josie's table so he could chat with his unmentionable wife.

Josie also may have run the Pearl Restaurant in Goldfield, but most of her time was spent searching for gold. Usually on horseback, and always alone, she relished riding through the pristine, almost silent, untouched countryside. Often she watched the dawn arrive before returning to town and work.

In 1910 Lane took a job as foreman of the Nevada United Mines in Ward, just south of Ely. Josie filed three gold claims during this time: the Nevada, Colorado, and Mexico. She also ran a boardinghouse and eventually managed the "elegant" Steptoe Hotel in Ely, which advertised five-course meals for the grand sum of $1.00. While she was working at the Steptoe, an article titled "A Woman Can Run a Hotel" appeared in a hotel blue book, lauding Josie's ability to manage such a fine establishment. She soon had another chance to prove herself as a capable and compassionate boardinghouse manager.

In October 1911, when "elegant" Mrs. Nathan Fay got off the train in Ely, she was ill prepared for the frigid cold and falling snow she encountered. Tired and hungry after traveling for days from Vermont to join her husband, who worked for the *White Pine News*, she wore only a light voile dress; her two sons were clad in short knickerbockers.

The threesome slipped and sloshed along the uneven board sidewalks. ". . . [T]he air was full of coal smoke . . . and I was shivering with cold," Mrs. Fay later recalled. Only an occasional dim light led their way to the Steptoe Hotel, where they arrived freezing, wet, and hungry. The warm, inviting dining room tables were set with pristine white linen tablecloths, and the delicious aroma that emanated from the kitchen almost made Mrs. Fay swoon from hunger.

When a woman came to greet them, Mrs. Fay was ready to turn herself and the boys over to the waitress's tender care. Instead, Josie Pearl almost shouted her disbelief upon seeing Mrs. Fay's attire. "Good God a mighty, girl, why didn't you wear some clothes?"

Poor, refined Mrs. Fay had "never heard a woman speak that kind of language and to me it was the end."

As the woman dissolved in a frosty puddle of tears, Josie quickly assessed the situation, gathered up the three distraught visitors, and settled them in a warm guest room. She plied them with hot food to soothe their shivering souls, and "assured me all would be well." Along with learning a few new words that day, Mrs. Fay never forgot Josie Pearl's kindness.

Josie became involved in the running of any town in which she landed. According to her biographer, she campaigned for Coloradoan Silas Frank during his run for Congress. After his victory, she attended the Republican National Convention in Pueblo, Colorado, to nominate William Howard Taft for president of the United States. In 1917 she helped introduce a bill in the Nevada State Legislature to revise pension laws for retired schoolteachers, giving them a sufficient income on which to live.

In the fall of 1918, an unwelcome Spanish visitor arrived in Nevada, riding across the country on a horse of death, striking without warning. The influenza pandemic of 1918–1919, commonly called the "Spanish flu" or the "Spanish lady" because of its origins, took the lives of more than twenty million people worldwide. No country was safe from the deadly scourge. Most of those stricken were, ironically, young and healthy; the old and weak were often spared. Lane Pearl encountered the Spanish lady and by November 20, 1918, he was dead.

Josie had no power over the diseased woman who fled with her husband of fifteen years. For a long time she lost interest in life itself, wandering from one mining town to another, in and out of Nevada and California, sometimes heading to Colorado and her family. She made a deposit on a rooming house in Tonopah, Nevada, but left before taking possession. Buying a cabin in

Searchlight, she stayed only a short while before drifting again. In the 1920s she opened the Pearl Inn in Bodie, California, and did some prospecting. She had the gold she uncovered melted into buttons, her "safety deposit box."

Back in northern Nevada by 1929, she managed a boardinghouse at the Betty O'Neal Mine near Battle Mountain. She later claimed to have "cleared $35,000 in three years—and then sunk the whole thing in another mine and lost it all. More than once I've been worth $100,000 one day and next day would be cooking in some ratty mining camp for $30 a month!"

She may have married a miner around this time, although she never mentioned this husband in later interviews. (There is also sketchy evidence she married once before meeting Lane Pearl.) She cooked for cowboys working on ranches in northern Humboldt County. In this desolate area, far from any town, frigid cold in winter and searing hot in summer, she finally found a place free of the ghosts of the past. Here Josie began prospecting full time, a profession that would shape her life for the next thirty years.

She donned overalls, sturdy shoes, and a sunbonnet, bought a burro she named Trampo, and loaded the unsuspecting beast with sacks of dried beans, sowbelly, coffee, and enough mining equipment to weigh the poor animal to the ground. Trampo moved only when motivated to do so and collapsed like a squashed bug when tired, gear scattering in every direction. When prospecting by automobile became possible, Josie bought a truck. Trampo was then allowed to move or squat whenever he wanted, and wherever he pleased.

She headed deep into the heart of Black Rock Desert, one of the most isolated regions in northern Nevada. Along with prospecting for gold, she searched for iron, manganese, copper, and nickel. Around 1934 she recorded her first claims. According to Schulmerich, "She slept where the night overtook her. She loved the little folks of the desert, the lizards, horned toads, little spotted skunk, rabbits, chipmunks, sage hens, larks, jay, and the mockingbird with his golden throat."

Although she thrived on the solitude of the desert, Josie also enjoyed the company of the few people she encountered. If she came across lonely prospectors like herself, she whipped out her crusty pots and pans and cooked up a mess of grub. Often down-and-out miners, even visitors touring the desert, stayed with her until they were ready to take off on their own again. After cooking for a couple of miners for some time in the Cove Canyon area, she was flabbergasted when they presented her with one of their own claims in gratitude, then helped her build a cabin near the mining site. She named her newly acquired mine the Juanita, and it kept her in supplies and provided her with some savings for many years.

During a particularly lean time, Josie went to work at a boardinghouse to earn extra cash, leaving the Juanita mine in the care of a watchman. Two men, with the help of her "trusty" guard, took over the little mine and plotted to kill her when she returned. With the help of friends, she rousted the claim jumpers and drove them off before they extracted any great quantities of ore from the Juanita.

During the depression of 1929 when the banks closed down, Josie lost all her profits from the Juanita. Never one to quit, she continued to haul ore from the mine and eventually sold it for $50,000.

Around 1933, on a trip to Albuquerque, New Mexico, to visit one of her sisters, Josie met journalist Ernie Pyle and invited him to visit her in the Black Rock Desert. Two years later Pyle showed up on her doorstep, and the two formed a friendship that lasted until Pyle's death on April 18, 1945, while serving as a correspondent during World War II. Writing of his encounter with Josie, Pyle found her:

. . . robust, medium-sized, happy-looking, and much younger than her years, which were sixty-some; there was no gray in her hair. Her dress was calico, with an apron over it; on her head was a farmer's straw hat, on her feet a mismated pair of men's shoes, and on her left hand and wrist—six thousand dollars' worth of diamonds! . . . Her cabin was the wildest hodgepodge of riches and rubbish I'd ever seen. The walls were thick with pinned-up letters from friends, assay receipts on ore, receipts from Montgomery Ward.

Josie kept a 30-30 rifle beside her bed. She owned a pump gun, a double-barreled shotgun, and an old single-shot .22, and claimed to have spent many sleepless nights with at least one of these weapons across her knees protecting her claims. She, however, was the real menace to be reckoned with on the roads around Winnemucca. Although Ernie Pyle dubbed her the "Tugboat Annie of the Desert," she looked more like a runaway bull as she plowed her old Ford truck down the middle of dirt roads, mowing down any sagebrush, creosote bush, coyote, or human in her path. "Here comes Josie," people shouted, "head for the brush!"

During the late 1930s Josie experienced a streak of bad luck with claim jumpers, unsuccessful partnerships, and wily men trying to steal her claims. She often spent valuable time traveling to and from Winnemucca embroiled in court hearings. On one trip during a terrible snowstorm, her car broke down. Accustomed to carrying heavy packs through twenty-below-zero temperatures, she set out on foot. After struggling through snowdrifts for miles, she was finally rescued by two men who stopped to help her. The good Samaritans were quite concerned when the elderly woman fell asleep as soon as her head hit the backseat of the car. "I'm all right, boys," she told the pair when she finally reawoke, "I'm a tough old bird."

When the trio realized they would not make their destination that night, they stopped at a nearby ranch house. Although the family there was ill with the flu, they allowed the strangers to stay, but not until the woman berated Josie for "running around with a bunch of men." Josie lit into the woman with a fire that ignited the frozen sky. "Woman," she blasted, "when you live miles from town you have to get to town with man, or woman, or the devil himself!" She then stayed and cared for the family until they were well. It was more than a month before she returned to her home and mines.

During World War II, Josie aided the war effort by prospecting for tin, tungsten, and molybdenum, ores needed to manufacture weapons. She gathered scrap—iron, aluminum, and rubber tires—and sold war bonds to everyone she knew. She spent a year working in a California hospital because of the shortage of nurses at home.

After the war, from about 1945 to 1951, Josie, now in her seventies, staked a slew of claims but sold none. "Gopher holes"—small claims not big enough to show promise—were all she could find. She did uncover a few opals and sold them to tourists and local jewelers in Winnemucca.

Josie experienced a degree of notoriety after Ernie Pyle's account of her life appeared in print. And although she did not like to be interviewed, author Nell Murbarger visited her in 1952 and found her surroundings much as Pyle had described them years earlier—ore samples piled helter-skelter in the yard of her ramshackle shack, car parts, pickaxes, pots, and pans littering the path to the front door. Josie was "neither friendly nor unfriendly," said Murbarger.

> [Her eyes] were shrewd and appraising; as steady as
> the eyes of a gunfighter, as inscrutable as those of

a poker player. . . . It was like looking at the last free antelope, or the last piece of open range. I felt instinctively that should she decide to move one of the surrounding mountains to the other side of the canyon, she would go about it calmly and deliberately, some evening after supper, perhaps. And she would move it—every stick and stone of it—and would ask no help from either God or man.

With no children of her own, Josie welcomed youngsters into her little house, kids needing and wanting to experience life in the rough. They helped with her claims, and she fed them well. Boys from age eight to fourteen, many from Winnemucca but also from as far away as Florida, came to hunt, fish, and prospect, often sleeping outdoors. She even taught some of them how to drive, much to the horror of her neighbors. Local ranchers gave her meats, fruits, and vegetables to help feed her hungry flock.

For many years she had dreamed of establishing an institution for disabled Nevada children. To be named for her late husband, the Pearl Foundation would require a slew of money—money that kept slipping out of Josie's hands. The big strike that would enable her to finance such a venture never appeared.

When Josie Pearl died in Reno, on December 29, 1962, at the age of eighty-nine, her death certificate listed her occupation as "hardrock miner." During her lifetime, she witnessed Nevada evolve from a dusty, sparsely populated state into a mecca where fortunes are won and lost within minutes. It's hard not to wonder what she must have thought of these instant millionaires after she struggled for so many years to acquire a small semblance of wealth, only to lose it again and again.

Josie Pearl was "a stalwart symbol and colorful figure of mining boom days," according to an article in the *Winnemucca Humboldt Star*, "linking the heritage of the pioneer past with present day progress." Of all the men and women Josie encountered over her four-score-plus years, none was more worthy of the term *elegant* than the lady in the calico dress with the pickax on her shoulder.

ANNE HENRIETTA MARTIN

1875–1951

Storming Political
(and Police) Barriers

The last place Anne Martin expected to be was sitting in a London jail waiting to be bailed out. Oh, she knew the chance she took when she helped hoist the 6-by-4-foot banner in front of the House of Commons, and whoever walloped the rather rude bobby on the head certainly had cause. "Black Friday," as November 18, 1910, came to be known, was certainly not starting out well for this Nevada native so far from home.

Anne's childhood gave little indication of the militant lifestyle she would choose—or maybe it did. Born to Louise Stadtmuller and William O'Hare Martin in Empire, Nevada, on September 30, 1875, and christened Anna Henrietta Martin, she was also called Annie, but Anne was the name she used after 1900.

Empire enjoyed enormous growth during the gold and silver strikes of the 1860s and '70s. Its proximity to the Carson River allowed for a lucrative lumber industry that provided necessary timber to downstream Virginia City mining communities. The tiny town had the distinction of being known as the seaport of Nevada.

1918

Vote for

ANNE MARTIN

Independent

For

United States Senate

NOMINATED BY NEARLY TEN
THOUSAND NEVADA VOTERS

Anne Henrietta Martin, Campaign Poster, 1918

William Martin was a partner in the Stadtmuller mercantile in Empire. His "soundness of judgment and human sympathy" secured his good standing in the community and led to his election to the Nevada Senate in 1875, the youngest man to reach this milestone. Anne adored her father, admiring his drive and ambition.

By 1880 Empire was withering along with the mining industry, leading the Martins to move to San Francisco, California. Five-year-old Anne was not at all happy about leaving Nevada and later wrote, "Child as I was, it was with a feeling of depression and foreboding that I left Nevada. . . ."

Fortunately her father must have felt the same, because after a few years the family returned to Reno. There Martin opened the W. O'H. Martin Mercantile Company and became a valued and wealthy member of the community.

In Reno, Anne attended Bishop Whitaker's School for Girls, established in 1876 and reputed to be the proper place for young women to enjoy the benefits of higher education while learning how "to fit themselves for womanhood, to purify the heart through culture of the mind." Not a particularly studious child, Anne preferred sports and tomfoolery to studies. In childhood diaries, she proudly detailed tricks she played on faculty members, such as the time she "let off a firecracker today in the schoolroom and Miss Pease rushed in and thought it was a door that slammed."

Biographer Anne Bail Howard described her as ". . . tomboy Annie who loved to climb trees and play softball, who loved her bicycle and rode astride her horse, who developed pictures on glass plates and made etchings—and played pranks at school."

Anne was a leader, an attribute that would serve her well in the years to come. It caused her nothing but trouble as a child, however, for she led her young cronies on one escapade after another. Her well-drawn caricatures relentlessly ridiculed her headmaster, the Reverend John R. Rankin. Unable to control the girls' boisterous pranks, he ordered the entire class of 1891 to repeat the school year. Anne refused and instead took the exams to enter Nevada State University. Passing with high marks, she entered college at the age of sixteen as a sophomore.

She found the challenge she was seeking at Nevada State University. Along with her studies, her love of sports blossomed. She won two state tennis championships while at the school.

After graduating, she attended Leland Stanford Junior University in California, obtaining a second bachelor's degree and a master's degree in history. Still infatuated with sports, she continued her championship tennis run while at Stanford.

Diplomas in hand, twenty-two-year-old Anne hurried back to Nevada in 1897 and accepted a teaching position at her alma mater, where she initiated and ran the Department of History. But when her father died in 1901, she left the university to handle family matters. The death of her father, plus the tragic drowning of a young man she was extremely fond of, may have provided the impetus she needed to explore beyond Nevada's borders.

Anne was experiencing a restlessness and discontent that was prevalent among young women across the country. Restricted by their mothers' Victorian morals, they were looking for new roads to travel as the twentieth century beckoned them. Anne chose to broaden her horizons by attending occasional classes at Columbia University in New York City. She traveled to Europe and the Orient, sometimes with friends, often content with her own company. She walked in and out of classes at Cambridge in England but concentrated on no particular curriculum. When she felt lonely, she parked herself at the London home of friends Lou and Herbert Hoover.

When she tired of England's cold, damp climate and yearned to watch the sun climb over Nevada's towering mountains or to feel the dry desert heat prickling her skin, she came home, occasionally teaching a course at the University of Nevada before wanderlust set in again. "Even in her later years," said Howard, "in spite of the wind and the cold she hated, Nevada called her."

In 1909 Anne Martin found the cause she was seeking, and it would shape the rest of her life. During her traveling years, she met women who shared her dysphoria with the restrictions society imposed on them. These women were ready to embrace the twentieth century, but first they would have to convince the rest of the world they were worthy, and capable, of doing so.

The desire to vote was the principal concern of women in the early 1900s. Since 1792 when Mary Wollstonecraft published her book *Vindication of the Rights of Women*, women had been seeking equality. In America suffragists Lucretia Mott, Elizabeth Cady Stanton, and Susan B. Anthony fought for more than fifty years for women's suffrage, culminating in the 1848 women's rights convention in Seneca Falls, New York. None of them lived to see women vote.

In London, Anne met suffragist Emmeline Pankhurst and her two daughters, Christabel and Sylvia, who ran the Women's Social and Political Union (WSPU), one of the most active, and volatile, organizations promoting women's rights. Tired of polite, "ladylike" strategies to obtain the vote, methods that had continually failed over the last fifty years, the Pankhursts orchestrated parades and demonstrations that often resulted in rock throwing and broken windows to call attention to the cause. By the time Anne joined the WSPU, they had the well-earned reputation as troublemakers. This probably delighted her independent, rebellious streak, and it wasn't long before her leadership abilities and boundless energy found her on platforms speaking before audiences advocating voting rights for women everywhere. When the November 18, 1910, demonstration took place, she was smack in the middle of the ruckus.

As the House of Commons readied to close for the Christmas holidays that year, the gathered gentlemen refused to consider, once again, the women's suffrage bill before them. A parade of women, some say numbering in the thousands, headed toward Parliament Square to protest the House's inaction. Banners swayed in the chilly London air; women sang and chanted as they neared Westminster Abbey. A barricade of constables blocked access to the House, and as Anne later wrote, "Police used bodies, elbows, and fists with great effect; great rough powerful men, they tossed us all, young and old, from one to the other, hurled, kicked, and knocked many down." She witnessed one "little nurse in uniform being knocked from one policeman to another."

Before the end of the day, women experienced abuses ranging from pinching to sexual assault. That night more than one hundred women languished in London jails, Anne Martin the only American arrested.

Luckily, she received only minor injuries from the two policemen who grabbed her and took her to the Cannon Row Police Station. She was charged with "obstructing the police in discharge of their duty." A fellow inmate's husband posted her bail.

The next day the female felons arrived for their hearing, suitcases in hand, ready to serve the jail time that would be imposed on them. Anne, however, showed up toting only her handbag and an umbrella, no luggage to see her through the upcoming imprisonment. The judge, most likely wearing a white powdered wig and curls, chastised the collection of women and released them, supposedly on orders from Home Secretary Winston Churchill, who would be running for reelection within a few months.

The notoriety of Anne's arrest spread through her home state like a rampaging herd of wild horses. The *Reno Evening Gazette* shouted the headline, "A Nevada Girl in London Jail," and quoted Anne's impression at the prospect of doing time:

I suddenly realized that in about an hour we should all be sentenced and driven off to Halloway jail in the Black Maria, which should be in waiting. I had brought nothing but my muff and an umbrella, and wondered what good the umbrella would do me in prison. The muff would be of use, as British prisons are very cold.

After her release, she returned to the States and was awarded the honor of carrying the Nevada banner in the 1911 New York City suffrage parade.

Anne learned a lot while enduring bullying bobbies on London streets. She had become a charismatic speaker and had fine-tuned the leadership abilities evident years before at Bishop Whitaker's School for Girls. She returned to Nevada to lead her state in the fight for women's rights.

Nevada women had not been idle while Anne Martin rallied in England. As early as 1869, the issue of a woman's right to vote was submitted to Nevada state lawmakers, and quickly tabled for future consideration. That December a Woman's Rights Ball was held at Bowers Mansion in Washoe Valley, an event the *Territorial Enterprise* deemed a "novelty" since it was run "from first to last" by women.

The suffrage amendment again appeared before the state legislature in 1871 and became an issue at twelve more legislative sessions before its passage. Women were definitely becoming more prevalent around Reno's Capitol grounds, as evidenced by the 1899–1901 General Appropriation Act that included a proposal for $300 to build and furnish the first ladies' restroom in the Capitol Building.

Anne joined the Nevada Equal Franchise Society and was soon elected press secretary, much to the chagrin of newspapers across the country. She deluged them with articles and flyers promoting the suffrage movement. By 1913 the *New York Times* was calling her "a spectacular figure among the suffragists." She was by then president of the society, and its membership had mushroomed.

Anne traveled across Nevada in rented Model T's to promote the movement. She could cover about 15 miles a day, all the poor vehicles could muster along sandy roads that sometimes disappeared without warning. The state encompassed about 110,000 square miles of sparsely populated communities, and she sometimes met with only a handful of ranchers or miners. She estimated she reached one voter for every 5 miles she traveled.

She waded through dust that turned to mud when winter rains hit southern Nevada. She tramped across the plains in the heat of summer and stood on bone-chilling street corners in northern Nevada with swirls of snow turning her soft brown hair old-age white. She knocked on stately mansion doors and dilapidated shack windows. Miners watched her descend underground to speak to those who could not leave work. She was not averse to sleeping out on the range if she failed to reach a nearby community by nightfall.

With Nevada's male:female population ratio at about 2:1, Anne endured her share of heckling by mainly male audiences, but nothing deterred the somewhat plumpish lady from speaking to whatever crowd assembled. "Women's place is in the home!" shouted saloon owners and patrons—both men and women—as she boldly strode through the swinging doors of a town's most popular establishment.

To the women who aided the suffrage cause, she issued a message of determination. "We are living in great and stirring times. Every Nevada woman who joins and lends her aid to the cause of equal suffrage is assisting constructive forces which will make the world a better place, will help to evolve the dream of one generation in the reality of the next."

Women had waited too long for equal standing in a country that prided itself on democracy for all. "When a democracy based on human instead of sex-rights is established," wrote Anne, "there will be less waste and destruction of human interest material by blind government Juggernauts which cannot see their goal, there will be more and more conservation of human and social forces, a greater usefulness and happiness for a far greater number."

Reno Evening Gazette editor George Wingfield fought adamantly against passage of the suffrage bill, vowing to leave the state if it passed. Liquor lobbyists, saloon and gambling hall owners, determined to keep Nevada an open state, feared a forceful women's vote would result in more temperance rules and regulations. Other publications such as the *Western Nevada Miner* and *Nevada State Journal* supported suffrage, some dubbing Anne and her colleagues "The Martinettes."

National suffragist Jane Addams lauded Anne's work in organizing the state's women. "Nevada was like a story in a book," she said. "So thoroughly was it organized that the girls could address almost every voter by his first name." Addams would be a staunch supporter of Anne's when she took on new challenges in a few years.

Election Day 1914 finally arrived. Nevada women surrounded polling places handing out last-minute flyers and keeping careful watch over the vote counting at the end of the day. Some states had experienced difficulties recording the yeas and nays on the women's rights issue. This time, however, Nevada approved the bill by 3,000 votes. Anne did not stop for congratulations—she had more work to do at the national level.

She embraced another militant suffrage organization, the National Woman's Party headed by Alice Paul, an outspoken suffragist who'd nearly starved to death while imprisoned for picketing the White House. As president, Anne organized one of the organization's largest demonstrations in 1917. By July of that year, however, she found herself facing jail time again for obstructing traffic by carrying the party's banner along a sidewalk near the White House. Biographer Howard pointed out that "[p]olice arrested the pickets, not the men who destroyed banners and mistreated the women. Sentences gradually grew from a few days to six months."

Anne defended herself by claiming it was the crowd that had assembled to watch the demonstrators that had obstructed traffic; she merely occupied a small area on a very wide sidewalk. "So long as you send women to prison for asking for justice," she argued during her court appearance, "so long will women be willing to go in such a cause."

She was found guilty, refused to pay the fine—as did all the arrested women—and was sentenced to sixty days in the Occoquan workhouse. Fortunately, she only served three days before an appeal freed the women.

As the suffrage campaign wound its way through the states, with Anne Martin nationally recognized as one of its most vocal proponents, she determined her next step was to run for the U.S. Senate. Until females sat in both Houses of Congress, she argued, "[w]omen will still be outside the pale of the real game of politics, and government, life itself, will still be controlled by men, who can administer the new laws practically as they please."

Although she would have preferred to form a strictly female party, as she believed existing political factions would not treat women fairly, she declared herself a candidate on the independent ticket in March 1918. She believed she was the first woman to run for Congress; however, a handful of women had already tossed their feathered hats into the political ring before Anne's candidacy.

Continuing her advocacy for women's rights, she enlisted the support of her friend, the suffragist Jane Addams, to help with her campaign. Longtime friend Dr. Margaret "Doc" Long of Denver served as Anne's driver across the vastness of Nevada and vowed to stay on the campaign trail "as long as I can and go to Hell or anywhere else . . ." Defeated in her first bid for a seat in Congress, Anne never questioned that she would run again.

In June 1919 the U.S. Senate passed the suffrage bill after President Woodrow Wilson finally gave his nod, and the House of Representatives narrowly approved it as well. But it was not until the following year, on August 26, 1920, that it was ratified by a majority of the states and became the Nineteenth Amendment to the Constitution.

The amendment contains just a handful of words, but to the women who battled for its passage, the number is immaterial to the power they hold. This is the statement Anne Henrietta Martin, and thousands like her, fought for years to have incorporated into the U.S. Constitution:

> The right of citizens of the United States to vote shall not be denied or abridged by the United States or by any State on account of sex. Congress shall have power to enforce this article by appropriate legislation.

The same year the amendment made its debut, Anne announced a second run for the U.S. Senate. Although she wanted to run on the Republican ticket, the party refused to endorse her, so she again entered the race as an independent. "I want to knock the fear out of the hearts of women," she wrote. "Even if I should not win, it will never seem so strange again when a woman tries it."

Declaring that "men legislators have protected property rights, women legislators will protect human rights," Anne berated a Congress that had appropriated $47 million to protect hogs, cattle, and crops from disease but had refused to help thousands of mothers and infants by denying $4 million to fight preventable diseases.

Anne and Doc Long headed out across the Nevada desert to recruit potential voters. Their trek turned out to be more eventful than they anticipated. Described in a 1920 article in the *Nevada State Journal*, the two middle-aged women drove out of Las Vegas toward the town of Ely, a distance of about 250 miles through rugged, undeveloped, and sparsely populated terrain. After several hours, they realized they had taken a wrong turn and driven at least 70 miles on the wrong road. The ladies were resigned to sleeping in the car for the night.

The next day, still lost after driving for hours, they spied a lowly shack occupied by a prospector, who invited them to dinner and allowed they could park their car near his cabin for the night. He also happened to know the way to Ely. The women finally arrived at their destination thirty-six hours late. Taking it all in stride, they continued across the state to the next campaign stop.

Once again, Anne was defeated in her bid for the Senate, and the grinding days of long campaigns and nights in strange places took a toll on her health. She moved to Carmel, California, but continued to maintain her voting rights in Nevada.

If she could not be heard as a member of Congress, Anne determined to educate her fellow Nevadans to its "position as the ugly duckling, the disappointment, the neglected stepchild, the weakling in the family of States, despite her charm and beauty and great natural advantages." In a 1922 article in *The Nation*, she blamed the livestock industry's monopoly over water rights for Nevada's woes, claiming the state would "continue to lie, inert and helpless, like an exhausted Titan in the sun—a beautiful desert of homeseekers' buried hopes" unless new, legitimate businesses and thriving, competing industries were invited to invest in it.

Anne Martin died in Carmel on April 15, 1951. Among her papers housed in the Bancroft Library at the University of California is a cache of poems she had written several years earlier while recuperating from a heart attack. One of them, "Home from Exile," leaves no doubt about her love of Nevada as she struggled to gain independence for its women and fought against its lack of progress. Although she is buried in California, the last stanza of the poem proves her heart and soul belong to Nevada.

> And what is this that knows the long, hard road I came?
> Oh, joy that I have come, and feel again!
> Enough this desert land, my native land,
> This dust, this earth in which my forbears lie,
> This wonder land of folk to be, is home.
> At last, at last, I have come home!

AH CUM KEE
1876–1929

Lady of the Land

*C*areful of them crates goin' to the St. Francis Hotel. You know how temperamental the chef gets at that ritzy place."

"What's so special about these Nevada shipments? Every time we get one into San Francisco, that chef just about drools over it."

"Don't you know? Them boxes contain white gold, Nevada sunshine."

"Man, what in the world you talkin' 'bout?"

"Them crates is full of white stringless celery, only grown in Nevada for the likes of those that stay at the St. Francis. I snitched a stalk once to see what all the fuss was about, and I'm tellin' you, that was the most delicious piece of celery I ever et. Mrs. Kee over in Hawthorne, Nevada, grows this stuff on her China Gardens farm. Seems she can't keep up with all the folks wantin' to et her special celery. Watch out now, here's the last box. Git your wagon down the road quick so's that chef don't come lookin' for us with his meat cleaver."

"Keep your shirt on, I'm movin' as fast as I can. Whoever heard of a piece of celery gittin' everyone so riled up?"

The chef at the St. Francis Hotel in San Francisco was not the only one who vied for Ah Cum Kee's special white celery. Elite establishments across the West also wanted to include the stringless delicacy on their menus and were willing to pay whatever price was asked to have her produce shipped across Nevada's desert terrain to grace the plates of their wealthy clientele.

Even though temperatures ranged from below freezing in the winter to above one hundred degrees during summer months, Ah Cum walked daily among the rows of her garden deep in the Nevada desert. She checked for stray weeds, stopping occasionally to pluck an intruder from its loamy bed. She scanned the fields of tomatoes, squash, and beans, keeping a watchful eye on a group of young workers several rows away. All six of her children could spot a willful weed or intruding critter as well as she could.

The children tiptoed along rows of shiny tin cans, silver shoots blossoming in the garden, reminiscent of the precious ores so sought after in the Nevada mountains. The metal containers shielded the white celery from the sun's rays, giving it the delicate flavor so sought after by the chefs who ordered her produce for their fancy hotels. One child lifted an old tomato can that covered a stalk while the next one scrutinized the ghostly stem to see if it was ripe for picking. Another sibling carefully watered each stalk individually before replacing the metal shield.

As she cradled a small tomato in her slender hands, Ah Cum checked for ripeness while peering under its leaves for the renegade bugs that thrived under the blistering southwestern sun. The chatter of her children floated over the fields as her thoughts drifted to her own far-off family, her mother and father who had long ago left her with a foster family and returned to China. She never knew why she was left behind—whether it was by choice or chance. A shadow of sadness crossed her face, but she had work to do and no time to dwell on the past. Shaking her head to obliterate those long-ago memories, she called her children to dinner and headed back across the fields.

Ah Cum Kee (center), *The Kee Family, Hawthorne, Nevada, 1907*

Long before Ah Cum was born, Nevada had established laws and rules governing the lives of its Chinese residents. The first Chinese arrived in the state around 1855 to dig ditches and canals along the Carson River, diverting water to the placer mines at Gold Canyon. Once the work was completed, the Chinese were allowed to remain but prohibited from mining Nevada's rich ore fields. Some went to work cutting and hauling lumber to the forbidden mines, while others set up laundries in existing mining towns, established Chinese restaurants, or started vegetable farms, peddling their goods in communities that sprang up along the Comstock.

An 1864 Gold Hill ordinance made it illegal for a Chinese person to live within 400 feet of a white individual unless given permission to do so. They could intermarry with Native Americans, Hispanics, and African Americans, but not whites. They could not testify in court. Chinese children were often not allowed to attend white public schools. The miles of railroad lines that crossed the Nevada desert utilized thousands of Chinese laborers, although no Chinese could ride in the passenger cars; they were relegated to the last car, the caboose.

Once the railroad was completed, white laborers who also worked on the railroads were as desperate as the Chinese to find employment. Fearing they would lose out to the vast number of unemployed Chinese who would work for much lower wages, mobs of angry whites stormed Chinese shantytowns, burning homes, sometimes maiming and killing any pigtailed alien in their destructive path. Those who survived were run out of town.

Although few Chinese women initially lived on the Comstock, those who did were relegated to the lowest status. "In the 1860s and 1870s," said historian Sue Fawn Chung, "the Euro-American population regarded most of the Chinese women as prostitutes." An 1875 law forced any Chinese woman entering the United States to prove otherwise. Only if she could convince port authorities she was married to a Chinese man already living in the States or was gainfully employed in a legitimate business would she be allowed to continue her journey. In 1882 an article in the *Carson City Morning Appeal* expressed the sentiments of the majority of white citizens in the West. "There are not a dozen respectable China-women on the coast, and the few that are here are never seen in the streets. In Carson there is not one of the latter class. The Chinese females here are all of the very lowest social order."

So when Ah Cum was born in Carson City in 1876, Nevada citizens did not welcome another Chinese female into their community.

Unlike the majority of Chinese families on the Comstock, however, Ah Cum's family enjoyed a modicum of success due to her father's business acumen. Non Chong Yee, who used the American name Sam Gibson, got his start as a woodcutter and eventually became a partner in Carson City's Quong Hing Company, which operated a mercantile and several boardinghouses for Chinese laborers. In addition, the Gibson family owned several buildings in Carson City. They dutifully paid required poll taxes and obeyed laws specifically designed for Chinese aliens.

Resentment against the Chinese increased when the Comstock began its downward economic spiral in the late 1800s. Whites boycotted Chinese-owned businesses, and Sam Gibson saw his entrepreneurial ventures evaporate. He soon feared for his family's safety and decided to return to China. Only Ah Cum was not included in the travel plans. As the family crossed the Nevada frontier to board a ship on the West Coast, they delivered their oldest daughter to a childless couple in Bodie, California, and continued their journey with their two younger children. Not fully understanding the enormity of her loss, Ah Cum watched her family disappear across the Nevada desert, never to see her parents again.

Why Ah Cum was left behind is still a mystery. The dutiful child accepted her fate, however, and even thrived under the care of her foster parents, Hong Wai Chang and his wife, Bitshee Ah Too. The couple ran a laundry in Bodie. Ah Cum learned how to speak, read, and write English, possibly attending school since she became quite expert in the language. To earn money, she baked and cooked for white families in the area, mastering the craft as she matured. Her expertise in the kitchen would serve her well over the years.

In 1888 Ah Cum and her foster parents moved to the small community of Hawthorne, Nevada, southeast of Carson City, where the couple found work in a local laundry. Two years later, when she was fourteen years old, Ah Cum married forty-three-year-old Chung Kee. Since arranged marriages were common among Chinese families, it's possible this union was preordained before her parents returned to China, and may be the reason she was left behind.

Chung Kee, whose birth name was Gee Wen Chung, and his partners operated the Chung Kee Company in Hawthorne, a mercantile specializing in Chinese goods such as tea leaves, candles, rice, salted eggs, and ginger, delivered from the San Francisco waterfronts. Whether Gee Wen Chung decided to change his name to Chung Kee to match that of the store, or he was so associated with the store that the name stuck as his own, has been lost in history.

Chung Kee owned a farm that supplied local citizens with fresh vegetables. His system of dry farming suited the arid temperatures of the Southwest, and he taught Paiute Indians his methods for producing a bountiful harvest. He ran a boarding-house for Chinese workers, and the fresh vittles he served were considered some of the best eating in town. Chinese laborers came to him for assistance in figuring out the taxes they were forced to pay. He helped them collect wages and send money to waiting families in China.

An 1890 article in the *Walker Lake Bulletin* announcing the nuptials of Ah Cum and Chung Kee touted the bride as "a pretty little Chinese damsel who can read, write and speak English like a native." Chung Kee, despite his astuteness in business, was described as "the heathen who propels a vegetable cart about town."

The Kee farm grew an abundance of vegetables, and they had no trouble selling the produce not consumed by their boardinghouse clientele. Chung Kee peddled his crops to Chinese laborers working the borax mines in the Candelaria area, while Ah Cum handled the cooking chores at the boardinghouse. The local newspaper listed the daily specials from the Kees' garden, and housewives eagerly watched for Chung Kee's horse-drawn wagon to rumble into town laden with luscious tomatoes, squash, and ripe fruit.

The Kees' specialty crop was white stringless celery, which thrived in the sandy, alkaline soil of the Nevada desert. Each tender sprout was placed beneath an empty tin can to prevent exposure to the sun, and then hand watered. The crispy albino stems were carefully picked, packaged, and shipped to elite hotels in Nevada, Utah, and California, including the elegant St. Francis Hotel in San Francisco.

Ah Cum and Chung Kee celebrated the birth of Ah Yen (Charles) in 1893, followed by daughters Al Lon (May) in 1895 and Ah Look (Florence) in 1897. Ah Cum's mastery of the English language, plus her husband's reputation as a fair trading man, helped solidify their standing in the Hawthorne community.

In 1901 Ah Moi (Myrtle) joined the family. Fon (Willie) was born in 1903, and Lin (Frank) arrived in 1906. Ah Cum prepared meals for boardinghouse patrons while keeping a watchful eye on her growing brood. Her cooking skills, particularly her baking expertise, became known throughout the community, and a group of hungry miners and merchants usually filed into her restaurant in anticipation of her sumptuous meals. After breakfast, workers lined up to purchase one of the boxed lunches she put together for them each day. Paiute Indians waited outside the kitchen door and traded nuts and herbs, intricately designed beadwork, and hand-woven baskets for a generous portion of Ah Cum's freshly baked bread. Using the bounty from the farm, she canned fruits and vegetables to serve her steady clientele. A family outing to nearby Walker Lake usually resulted in fresh fish on the menu that night for her restaurant customers.

Few Chinese families lived in the area, and the Kees had no extended family upon which to rely, but they enjoyed a relatively peaceful relationship with the white Hawthorne community. Chung Kee's daily bounty of luscious produce, plus Ah Cum's fluency in English and her expertise in the kitchen, certainly contributed to the family's acceptance.

Unlike other parts of Nevada that still refused to allow Chinese to be educated alongside white children, Hawthorne allowed the Kee children to attend the local school. Initially teased for wearing traditional Chinese clothing and braiding their hair in queues, they quickly adopted American styles, and it was probably during their school years that they acquired their American names. Ah Cum also chose to wear Western clothing at a time when many Chinese still wore wide-legged cotton pants, black smocks, and slippers. As Chinese women such as Ah Cum Kee adapted to American dress and customs, white women were discovering the rich, delicate artistry of Oriental furnishings. According to writers Cathy Luchetti and Carol Olwell:

> The closer Chinese women came to keeping an orderly, Western household with flowers at the window and a freshly washed floor, the more they were accepted by the American women. Ironically, these same women often filled their own over-

crowded Victorian homes with carved jade, Tang jars, and the scent of joss—the elements that they tried to discourage in the houses of their Chinese converts.

In June 1909 sixty-three-year-old Chung Kee died, leaving Ah Cum to support six youngsters ranging in age from three to sixteen. The older children helped with harvesting the produce grown on their "China Gardens" farm, a term used throughout the West to distinguish Chinese farmland. The 1910 census listed Ah Cum Kee as the only Chinese female farmer in Nevada, with her assets valued at around $1,000, equivalent to about $20,000 today. Although she employed hired hands when needed, it was her own sweat, and that of her children, that brought in the fruits and vegetables and planted the seeds for next year's crop, special care being given to those stark white celery stalks.

When the Southern Pacific Railroad bypassed Hawthorne, the town's decline was inevitable. By 1912 the population had diminished to the point that Ah Cum found it difficult to fill her boardinghouse with hungry customers. With half a dozen children to feed and clothe, she went to work as a boardinghouse cook in the dusty town of Tonopah. She retained her land in Hawthorne and leased it during her absence.

Around 1914 a relative proposed to take Ah Cum's son Charles and her older daughters, probably May and Florence, to China to arrange marriages with Chinese natives. Ah Cum went to San Francisco to obtain the necessary documents for their travel. But before they could board the ship, she changed her mind: Charles was twenty-one years old and could go if he wished, but she refused to send her daughters. Charles left for China, where he married; he eventually returned to America without his wife, and served in the army during World War I.

In 1915, when Ah Cum's daughter Florence decided to marry a white man, interracial marriages were still outlawed in both Nevada and California. The couple set sail and anchored just far enough off the California coast for the ceremony to take place in international waters. Florence only lived a few more years, succumbing during the influenza epidemic of 1918–1919.

Because she had been forced to earn her own way in the world at an early age, Ah Cum could not afford to subscribe to many of the Chinese customs imposed on women such as never traveling alone or being seen outside the home without an escort. During her years as a single woman struggling to hold her family together, she boldly boarded buckboards, stages, and trains, rarely experiencing the discrimination and disparaging remarks of unthinking white passengers. Her Western dress and ability to speak fluent English probably saw her through more than one unpleasant situation. Ah Cum Kee quietly, but determinedly, paved the way for the next generation of Chinese women to enter the American West with heads held high, not bowing to any master.

Sometime after 1912, Ah Cum went to work for Louie King, a Tonopah restaurant owner, hog raiser, and manager of a handful of "ladies" in the red light district. She and King never married, but in 1916, at the age of forty, she gave birth to a daughter, Nellie.

The relationship between Ah Cum and Louie King was destined for doom. He wanted a traditional Chinese wife—actually more than one wife, as was the Chinese custom, all of them obedient and subservient. Ah Cum refused to play the role of the dutiful Chinese spouse. When his insistence on her servitude escalated into tirades that flared and waned according to the temperature of the day—and Tonopah was a very hot town—she returned to Hawthorne with her young children and infant Nellie.

Ah Cum discovered Hawthorne virtually a ghost town. Where once crowds of hungry prospectors and merchants had waited outside her restaurant door, empty boarded-up buildings now dotted the landscape much like the tin can covers that were once sprinkled across her farmland.

Scanning the rows of dilapidated buildings, she realized her source of income lay in what others saw as rotting wood. Hiring local Paiute Indians to tear down the abandoned hovels, she sold the lumber to nearby mining operations. The business, however, lasted only as long as the wood did. With few buildings left to dismantle, she moved her family to Reno and reluctantly went back to work for Louie King, who now owned a restaurant and herb shop along with running a handful of pleasure houses. King eventually returned to China a rich man and acquired three wives.

Ah Cum stayed in Reno until 1925, when she moved to Oakland, California, to be near her youngest son, Frank. She lived her final days at peace with a world that had considered her lower than the rats that scavenged the piers of San Francisco or the snakes that hissed and crawled across the hot barren Nevada desert. As she freely walked along the streets of Oakland without fear of being spat upon or the subject of some ribald racial joke, she may have wondered what horrible fate could have befallen her so many years ago when her parents abandoned her. Her happier memories, however, dwelled on the days in the Nevada fields when her children romped between the rows of plump vegetables pulling up those white, ghostly celery stalks so precious to western dining establishments.

Her death in 1929 was left unmentioned in the local newspaper. Yet a wealth of people from the Nevada desert to the California shores remembered the beautiful woman who spoke so well yet was more than willing to bend her back and work the land to give her children a place to call home.

Maude Frazier

1881–1963

Education Reformer

"Coming from a family of teachers," said Maude Frazier, "I was expected to follow the tradition. Yet I was cast in the wrong mold to fit comfortably as a teacher of that period." Rather than adhering to a prim and proper lifestyle and following the rules and regulations imposed on teachers in the early 1900s, Maude preferred a brisk bicycle ride across town or a speedy gallop out over the Nevada desert. Maude Frazier bent and broke the rules of feminine comportment, but her visionary insights into the educational needs of rural Nevada schoolchildren made her a pioneer in Nevada education.

Maude was born on April 4, 1881, in rural Sauk County, Wisconsin. Like many children, she loved playing in the attic amid discarded family relics, probably imagining great adventures and undiscovered lands. When she happened upon a cache of her grandfather's papers hidden under years of dust and debris, detailing his adventures as he migrated into the Northwest Territory, she realized her wanderlust longings were inherited and not strange ideas that only she harbored. In later years she remembered her many hours spent rummaging through attic antiques and lamented

Maude Frazier

that today's children would never know the secrets and untold stories languishing in corners of ancient dormers. "As the years pass, I keep thinking that our greatest lack today is <u>attics</u>. Modern homes never have them, with the result that young people live only in their own generation, feeling no intimate connection with the past. Their roots will go deeper if their homes have attics!"

Reluctantly obeying her parents' wishes that she become a teacher, Maude attended Wisconsin Normal School in Stevens Point, Wisconsin. After passing the teaching examination, she taught in small Wisconsin timber towns and iron-mining communities. In these economically depressed districts, she first encountered children eager to learn but lacking the tools and teachers to do so, something she never forgot as she made her way beyond rural Wisconsin fields.

To supplement her meager teacher's salary, Maude worked a variety of jobs. In her autobiography, she remembered clerking in country stores and taking in sewing. The day she spilled ink on the only skirt she owned forced her to develop a more creative bent. She dyed the rest of the skirt to match the inkblot and proudly considered herself lucky to now own a brand-new black skirt.

Unfortunately, Maude's yearning for great adventures did not fit the demeanor expected of a proper schoolmarm in the early 1900s. She preferred to play ball rather than watch. She enjoyed ice-skating and swimming, activities frowned upon by staid school board members, almost always men. Even upswept hairdos and bright-colored dresses adorned with too many ruffles could lead to a distressed look or disciplinary action. Although Maude looked every bit the schoolteacher in her neatly coiffed hairdo and rimmed eyeglasses, she chafed under the scrutiny and demands placed upon women in general and teachers specifically. "It is quite possible that it was never intended by the good Lord that I should be a schoolteacher. At least not so soon after the turn of the Twentieth

Century, when they were definitely a distinct species." For the rest of her life, she bristled under the scrutiny of male supervisors, whether it be regarding her dress, her demeanor, or her recommendations for education reform.

Maude often remembered her grandfather's words, and she yearned to explore new worlds and experience great adventures. Because she was already chafing under the latest Wisconsin rules imposed upon teachers—restrictions against dancing and playing cards at any time—she pored over newspaper articles describing the rush for gold in the West. Newly formed mining communities begged teachers to come and educate their children. Female teachers who first went west were often dismissed if they married, and with so few marriageable women in the barren outback of America, it wasn't long after their arrival that they met and married a love-starved rancher, cowboy, or prospector. A 1901 article in the *Tonopah Bonanza* newspaper claimed that twenty applicants had applied for a teaching position but the school board was looking for an "old maid," hoping she would stay longer than some of the previous women who had taken the job, only to be swept away to a preacher within months of their arrival.

Maude applied for teaching positions in several far-off territories, turning down an opportunity in Alaska before accepting a job in Genoa, Nevada, in 1906. With trepidation, her parents put her on the train, probably expecting she would be scalped before reaching her destination. She arrived safely, however, and began a career that would fulfill her desire to provide learning-starved, impoverished children with a meaningful education.

Maude was the first to admit she made mistakes while learning her trade, but she was surprised when school board members criticized her for riding her bicycle around town, ". . . something," she said, "which no nice girl would think of doing. Their objection to such a means of getting about always appeared incongruous to me, since the board members expect this same dignified teacher to perform all the undignified tasks of janitor work" for the grand sum of $22 a month.

> In those early years of my teaching career, I did discover that there was nothing to compare with this janitor work to let off steam which had arisen from anger. Taking out one's ire on broom or mop really makes the dirt fly! I had plenty of reasons to need this physical exertion.

Along with the majority of schoolteachers in the early 1900s, Maude was expected to handle situations far beyond her teaching duties. She had to locate books, paper, pencils, and slates for her pupils; cut and carry wood for the stove; tote the drinking water from sometimes far-off streams; and sweep and scrub the schoolhouse floor, if the schoolhouse was fortunate enough to have a floor.

Teachers in Nevada dealt with floods and fires, stampeding cattle and runaway horses, raiding Indians, drunken cowboys, outlaws, and down-and-out prospectors. Snakes, scorpions, coyotes, and other strange desert creatures greeted Maude upon her arrival. She was a novice in the desert, unsure whom to trust or how far to wander.

When she entered the Genoa schoolhouse, there was not a book to be found. Children brought materials from home, and Maude utilized this assortment of teaching tools as best she could. Her charges ranged in age from five to fifteen, and their educational background was just as diverse. She taught children who eagerly wanted to learn and those who would rather be riding the range or searching for ore in the mining fields.

Maude traveled to some of the most remote areas of Nevada,

teaching whoever showed up at whatever school facility available. In Dinero Gorge, she held classes in a tent with no supplies. Lovelock and Goldfield, both prosperous districts, provided ample school materials, including a piano. In Seven Troughs, about 30 miles from Lovelock, a tent school sufficed until a brothel was moved to make way for a roughly constructed schoolhouse. Even then, floorboards were spaced so far apart that dropped pencils had to be retrieved from under the building. In winter Maude and the children wore layers of clothing and huddled under blankets brought from home to keep warm. She taught in temperatures from below zero to more than a hundred degrees and found that most of her students seldom complained and rarely missed school—so great was their desire to learn. The lack of materials was a nuisance, but Maude soon realized that a "good school is a thing of the mind and spirit and not a thing of gadgets."

During summer breaks, she learned to ride and could often been seen tearing on horseback across the range amid a herd of cowboys, her six-foot frame sitting tall in the saddle.

For sixteen years Maude tended to the educational needs of western Nevada children. During the summers of 1918 through 1920, she attended school at the University of Nevada in Reno. In 1920 her exemplary work at the university afforded her the opportunity to become principal in Sparks, Nevada. When she tried to rent a room in Sparks, however, the landlady told her, "Do you think I have sunk so low that I would rent a room to a woman? Especially a woman teacher?"

The following year, she applied for a job in Las Vegas as deputy superintendent with the Nevada Department of Education. Maude at first viewed the sparsely populated community with skepticism, claiming it "was the most unprepossessing place I had ever seen, and nobody at that time could have convinced me that I would ever come to love it as I eventually did. It became dearer to me than any other spot on earth."

The four men who had previously held the position of deputy superintendent declared no one could traipse across such a vast desolate terrain and live to tell about it. The area consisted of more than 40,000 square miles, all of which Maude had to travel alone. The first thing she did was buy an old Dodge car she dubbed Teddy, for Teddy Roosevelt "because it was such a rough rider." After a few lessons in auto mechanics, she and Teddy headed out to visit the schools within her immense jurisdiction.

> Teddy and I became a team as we covered the trails. Garage men were our friends. They drew crude maps on any scrap of paper available, listed landmarks along the way, made lists of supplies and equipment I must carry. I would need a shovel, an axe, tow ropes, two jacks, good tire pump, canteens of water, gas and oil. Neither must I ever be without an abundance of canned goods, which in turn necessitated a can opener. A bundle of wiping rags and a blanket completed the requirements.

To her supplies she added canned tomatoes, two flashlights, magazines, and a deck of cards.

Teddy cooperated as much as possible, but occasionally even the old workhorse could not get out of the sifting sand that sometimes rose above its hubcaps. Maude would let the air out of Teddy's rear tires, making it easier to ride atop the sand. After the Dodge gained its footing again, she would pump the tires back up before continuing her journey. Sometimes she and Teddy languished for hours surrounded by a storm of dust before she could see well enough to drive.

Although warned about the dangers lurking in the desert—absolutely no road signs to guide her (in fact, few roads), wild animals, snakes, and even more perilous and unfriendly human predators—she encountered none. Strangers stopped to help if Teddy struggled and sank in the sand. They offered her water, food, even a place to stay if darkness fell before she reached her destination. She never felt afraid and actually enjoyed the solitude, relishing "the ever-changing lights and shadows on the far mountains, the gorgeous desert flora—cacti, Joshua trees, Spanish dagger—an occasional friendly coyote, the vivid sunsets, the clean smells of the desert, and of course Teddy, ready to do his best."

As she traveled unmarked trails, she remembered the four superintendents who preceded her. "Every time I would stop to wipe my brow and rest my back, I would think of those men and how they would laugh if they could see me now, and thus I derived energy to attack my job again."

The time Maude had spent teaching in rural schools, and now as deputy superintendent, reinforced her conviction that the most talented teachers should be sent to the most remote regions. These areas, she claimed, needed teachers who could handle unexpected situations without relying on superiors for guidance. They must know something about a wide range of subjects from math to history to foreign affairs, and be able to provide social as well as educational stimuli so their charges would grow both academically and communicatively. She lauded one such teacher who impressed her by using what was on hand—jars filled with scorpions and spiders to teach biology, plus a resident snake that was allowed to roam freely about the classroom to keep the mouse population at bay. "To me," said Maude, "she was a perfect example of making teaching fit the community."

Although she tried to implement improvements in schools under her jurisdiction, her position carried little weight with local school board constituents, who preferred making their own decisions and were not impressed with the lady agitator. When she attended staff meetings with the state superintendent and his all-male staff, they let her know they resented the presence of a woman within their domain. "I was well aware," she said, "that when a woman takes over work done by a man, she has to do it better, has more of it to do, and usually for less pay."

When a new superintendent was elected in 1926, Maude lost her position as deputy. In 1927 she ran for and won the position of Clark County school superintendent, which included the Las Vegas school district. At the time, Las Vegas had two elementary schools and one very dilapidated high school. Also taking on the task of high school principal, Maude urged the people of Las Vegas to build a new high school before the old one collapsed. With a city population of less than 3,000, she had her work cut out for her in pushing through a bond issue to provide funds for a new school, but two events helped win her cause: Las Vegas experienced a population explosion when construction began on the Hoover Dam 30 miles south of the city, and the ancient school building finally met its demise in a devastating fire.

Las Vegas schools thrived under Maude's direction, so much so that by 1946 she proposed a statewide reorganization of the school system. She had never forgotten the children she first taught in the isolated rural communities of Wisconsin and Nevada, and she still hoped to provide them with better teachers and a decent education.

To accomplish her lofty educational goals, Maude, at the age of sixty-seven, ran for an assembly seat in the Nevada State Legislature. Losing in her first attempt, she ran again in 1950 and succeeded to the assembly, where she served for the next twelve years. Once gaining leadership of the Education Committee, Maude set about redesigning the state school system, a task that took her ten years. As one legislator recalled, Maude did her homework. "She knew to the penny how much money was available, knew by heart how many students would be affected by a bill."

During her legislative terms, Maude saw many of the suggestions she had first proposed in the 1920s to improve Nevada schools come to fruition. More than 200 school districts were consolidated into seventeen county districts, teachers' salaries and facilities were standardized, tax bills were passed to fund schools. Along with her drive for better school standards, she found time to work on and helped pass the first civil rights bill in 1959.

Once she had straightened out the Nevada school system, Maude set her hat toward developing a southern division of the University of Nevada.

Established in Elko in 1874, the University of Nevada was relocated to Reno in 1886. Maude urged the legislature to institute a southern campus to serve the educational needs of Las Vegas and surrounding communities. Concerned about diminishing the student base in Reno, the legislature grudgingly agreed to fund $200,000 for a Las Vegas branch of the university, but residents would have to foot the additional $100,000 needed for its construction.

Maude knew where to find the money. By 1955 gambling and star-studded shows permeated the Las Vegas Strip, even though the town had yet to reach its height of celebrity. Maude and a handful of enthusiastic citizens took their cause to the people who had the money and the power. They enlisted the aid of club owners, singers, and dancers, along with educators and civic leaders. Together they organized a telecast to help raise the necessary funds. Her hard worked paid off in April 1956 when she was handed a shovel to dig the first spadeful of earth establishing Nevada Southern University, the southern campus of the University of Nevada.

The first university building was named Maude Frazier Hall. No one was prouder of that school than the lady who had maneuvered her way across the open desert in old Teddy to provide an education for the rural children of southern Nevada.

In 1962, Maude broke her hip, but nothing as insignificant as a broken bone could stop an eighty-one-year-old tomboy like Maude Frazier. Maneuvering her crutches through legislative halls, she accepted the position of lieutenant governor when Governor Grant Sawyer asked her to fulfill the term of Rex Bell, who had died suddenly. For six months she reigned as the first woman to hold one of the most prestigious positions in Nevada government.

Her crippled old hip never healed properly, and Maude was soon relegated to a wheelchair. But even that did not stop her from doing whatever she wanted. Brent Adams, a Washoe County district judge, loved to tell the story of how he watched her cook chicken by setting a bowl of flour on the floor next to her wheelchair, dropping the chicken into the flour, and then tossing it across the room to a waiting frying pan.

The one thing Maude could not control was time, and time finally ran out for the lady educator and legislator on June 20, 1963, at the age of eighty-two. No one had made more of an impact on the education of children in Nevada than Maude Frazier. Her relentless pursuit of better schools and better education made her a figurehead among Nevada educators. She considered herself a "desert rat" but wanted more than dust-filled classrooms for the students she found in run-down schools. Because her ideas differed from those expected of female schoolteachers of her day, because she chose to ride bicycles and roam the desert alone and unafraid, and because she tackled jobs considered "man's work," she wanted more than anything to impress upon children that

. . . they must not be afraid to be different. We turn

out people who know the same things, do the same things, think the same way. Yet it has been the non-conformists, the people who dared to be different, who dared to experiment with new ideas, who have contributed most to the world—the Edisons, the Wrights, the Marconis.

And even though early in her career she questioned her decision to teach, she also promised, "If I was going to be a teacher I was going to be a good one." That she definitely accomplished.

FELICE COHN
1884–1961

An Independent Spirit

A crispness in the predawn air held the promise of autumn as eleven-year-old Felice Cohn leaped out of bed to greet the beginning of a new school term. Dressing quickly and hurrying through breakfast, much to her mother's consternation, she double-checked her supplies just as she had every day for the last week in preparation for this day: books, tablets, pencils, chalk, ruler—everything in order. Grabbing her schoolbag, she made the rounds of good-byes. Mama and Papa Cohn received quick kisses, but Grandpa Sheyer demanded his usual bear hug before she made her escape out the door.

Felice ignored her friends playing in the schoolyard and hurried inside the small building, straight to the teacher's desk. She carefully laid out her supplies and sat down in the huge chair that dwarfed her tiny frame. As she struggled to see over the equally intimidating desk, she resembled a delicate figurine ready to break into smithereens if someone said an unkind word.

She nervously waited as the students trickled into the schoolroom, giggling and pointing at their confused schoolmate who didn't seem to know she was in the wrong seat. Although she wished for

Felice Cohn

silence, the children continued their ribald antics as she struggled out of the large chair and stood before the class. She began to call the roll. Her friends answered with boisterous chants: "Present, Teach!" "You're going to get in so much trouble, Felice." "Stop pretending you're the schoolmarm." But Felice wasn't playacting or fooling around—she would be their teacher for the entire year.

A shortage of educators probably led to young Felice Cohn's first endeavor as a schoolteacher, and it's almost certain she endured a fair share of teasing and other abuse at the hands of her students. Some of her pupils towered over her, and the bigger boys often relished picking up their petite teacher and spinning her around the playground.

Although Felice may have enjoyed some aspects of her first teaching job, she soon realized that with additional education, she could accomplish much more than the little schoolhouse had to offer. Her parents agreed.

One of five children, Felice was born in Carson City, Nevada, on May 14, 1884, to Morris and Pauline Sheyer Cohn. The Cohns owned several thousand acres of land in the Carson Valley and Tahoe areas, and Morris is credited with introducing alfalfa to Nevada, plus establishing the first creamery in the state. His interest in mining would influence Felice's chosen career in the years to come. Her grandfather Rabbi Jacob Sheyer had been a respected member of the community for many years, and the buttons almost popped off his suit with pride when he saw his young granddaughter teaching school. He knew she was destined for greatness.

When the Cohns realized early on that their daughter possessed an exceptional mind, particularly after receiving her first teaching certificate at the age of eleven, they encouraged her in whatever endeavors she chose to pursue. Felice initially considered entering the medical field—probably greatly encouraged by her eleven great-uncles, who were all practicing physicians—but she chose instead to concentrate on the law when she "decided she would rather argue than prescribe."

After her short stint as a schoolteacher, she continued her education at Reno's University of Nevada. Never one to let time pass unrewarded, she also attended Nevada Business College and Leland Stanford University in California. In 1902 Felice walked out of Washington Law School in St. Louis, Missouri, with a law degree in her hands. She had just turned eighteen years old.

Returning to Carson City, Felice was admitted to practice law in the state of Nevada on June 17, 1902. Only the fifth woman admitted to practice in Nevada, she was the first with a law degree. At the time she also had the distinction of being the youngest person ever accepted by the Nevada State Bar.

Of the women who preceded Felice in obtaining recognition by the state to practice law, none was a Nevada native, and few had any formal legal training. Similar to many of their male counterparts, they lacked degrees from established law schools. The assumption for many years had been that any male over the age of twenty-one, of sound moral character, and capable of passing an examination overseen by a judge, could announce his intention of opening a law business. Not until 1893 were females allowed the same privilege.

From the outset Felice had an office full of clients. Her father's early interest in mining led her to concentrate her legal expertise on land issues and mining cases, both compelling concerns in the early days of twentieth-century Nevada. With new discoveries of gold and silver outcroppings in the Tonopah area, Nevada was bouncing back from a twenty-year depression. As miners sought riches comparable to the 1859 Comstock bonanza, and speculators rushed to buy up what they anticipated would be lucrative acreage, the state enjoyed a resurgence of population and wealth. Felice was in the throes of new issues involving modern-day mining and land distribution. She astutely chose to open offices in the mining districts of Carson City and Goldfield.

Although the stigma against women in the legal field was boldly evident in a *Goldfield News* article, it was also apparent Nevada's new lady lawyer created quite a stir:

> Miss Cohn is a slender woman of average height, with dark hair and liquid black eyes which flash with interest as she talks. There is nothing about her appearance or manner to suggest that she is at all masculine nor does her simple white costume have anything about it to suggest that she has ceased to be a woman in becoming a lawyer.

Advancements came quickly to Felice. She became the first woman U.S. assistant district attorney in 1906, a position she held for eight years. Two years later she was admitted to practice before the U.S. District Court of Appeals in San Francisco.

A twist of events in 1907 found Felice demoting herself to the job of court reporter for a complicated case before the district court of Ormsby County, Nevada. Why such a successful woman attorney would agree to serve in this lesser capacity is open to argument. In all probability, she was asked to accept the position because she was the one person who could sort through and compile the mass of evidence presented during the four-year State Bank and Trust Company case, one of the longest trials in Nevada history. One individual testified for more than 145 days, all of which Felice recorded. She would continue to serve as court reporter for the first judicial district for eight years while continuing to run her law practice.

When Nevada women took up the cause for the right to vote, Felice led a group of quiet but persistent voices in the battle for equality. Unlike her peer and fellow Nevadan Anne Henrietta Martin, a fierce and often outspoken advocate of the suffrage movement, Felice preferred more peaceful means of arguing for women's rights. A 1913 national magazine compared the campaigning skills of the two Nevada women and noted that "like the great majority of woman suffragists in this county, [Felice Cohn] does not believe in militant methods." She was one of the founders of the Equal Suffrage Society and the Nevada Voters' Club, both nonviolent suffrage organizations.

She spoke before the Nevada legislature in 1911 proposing a resolution for women's voting rights. Her words were those that would eventually be used in the state's proclamation. Short and direct, her statement rings as strongly today as it did almost one hundred years ago: "There shall be no denial of the elective franchise at any election on the account of sex."

Although she never married, Felice chose to involve herself with the welfare of Nevada's women and children. As her law practice grew, she took on innumerable divorce cases and witnessed the devastation and poverty suffered by displaced wives and forgotten youngsters. She fought to pass child labor laws, establish foster homes, and create fair adoption proceedings, issues that adversely affected all women and children regardless of their family status.

She favored Nevada's short-term, liberal divorce statutes. "Nevada has been criticized for her divorce laws," she argued. "But it is due almost entirely to the need of relief by the citizens of other states that we find ourselves the 'cure' center of the world." Women who were restricted from obtaining divorces in their own states flocked to Nevada to free themselves from marriages that might otherwise leave them trapped in incompatible, sometimes violent unions.

During World War I, Felice relinquished her law practice in Nevada to become a special attorney in charge of land sales for the U.S. government. Her expertise in mining and land issues was becoming nationally recognized.

In March 1916 Felice Cohn was admitted to practice before the U.S. Supreme Court, only the fourth woman accepted into that august assembly. When President Woodrow Wilson met her at a reception in Washington, DC, he commended her for achieving a status few women had realized up to that time. He then kept the cream of Washington society waiting as he lingered to chat with the newly crowned Supreme Court attorney.

Reno newspapers noted Felice was becoming "the center of attraction" in Washington society. She enjoyed the parties and particularly the political activity that surrounded her as she traveled back and forth between Nevada and the nation's capital with her government job.

In 1918, as a hearings attorney for the U.S. Land Office, a job she undertook after her stint as a land sales attorney, she handled cases involving land fraud in Nevada, Colorado, Kansas, and Oklahoma. When she resigned in 1922, by her own admission, she "succeeded in having more than 80,000 acres of mineral land restored to the public domain." She was the first woman to hold this position, and it took four men to replace her when she left.

In 1921 Felice reopened her law office in Reno, but she really wanted to explore her options in politics. She ran for an assembly seat in the Nevada State Legislature in 1924 but lost the election.

New legal challenges soon occupied her when she received an appointment as a bankruptcy referee for the state of Nevada, a role she held until 1934. Again, she was the first woman to attain the position. During her tenure, only two of her decisions were reversed—an unprecedented record. When her last term expired, her experience afforded her the opportunity to serve as national chairman of the Committee on Ethics of the National Association of Referees in Bankruptcy.

Felice again tried her hand at politics in 1927, running for Reno city attorney. No matter how high their regard for her work, however, voters seemed to prefer she stay in her law office and not enter the political fray. She watched from the wings as more and more women sought the challenges politics offered, and her desire to join them showed strongly in an essay she penned titled "Women of Nevada Interested In Politics":

> . . . [N]o matter how varied our tastes may be; no matter whether we be homemakers or business women, or perhaps both (for we frequently combine these talents); no matter whether we be young or old, rich or poor, active or ailing, we have one great interest that appeals to us all. We are all sisters under the skin. There is one clarion call that we all respond to and one topic of conversation that never grows old or stale or loses interest, and that is Politics! Yes, Politics—capital "P" at that!

Because Felice believed women should help themselves, she involved herself in establishing organizations that benefited their advancement both at home and in the workplace. She was one of the founding members of the Nevada Equal Franchise Society, a founder and first state president of the Nevada Federation of Business and Professional Women's Clubs, and president of the Reno Business and Professional Women's Club.

Within the legal field, she served as regional director and vice president for the National Association of Women Lawyers, was on the general council of the American Bar Association, and served as vice president of the American Bar Association for Nevada. She was also active in the Nevada State Bar Association and Washoe County Bar Association. In all, Felice was admitted to practice law in the states of Nevada, California, Colorado, and the U.S. Supreme Court.

The *Nevada State Journal* noted in 1932 that with all the work and activities she took on, ". . . she still finds time to assist those organizations which sponsor welfare work and interest among all peoples." She served on the state advisory board of the American Red Cross during World War II, the only woman on the board. Twice she chaired the Washoe County Red Cross, and also served on the board of the Reno chapter of the Young Women's Christian Association. "With women taking their place in world affairs as they are today," the *Journal* article continued, "and with Felice Cohn's background we dare not venture an opinion as to how far this outstanding daughter of Nevada may go."

Through her efforts, the Nevada Historical Society received a state grant to assist in establishing a permanent site in Reno. And in 1950 the Nevada Federation of Business and Professional Women's Clubs recognized her numerous achievements and unstinting efforts to create a state where women would be respected and heard by naming her Outstanding Woman for the State of Nevada.

Hoping her reign as Nevada's woman of the year would make a difference, she relinquished an opportunity to go to Europe to attend a conference of the International Association of Women Lawyers to involve herself once again in Nevada politics. In 1950 she ran for Washoe district judge, but faced defeat for the third time. Felice excelled in her role as an astute attorney and advocate for women's rights, overcoming and overlooking numerous obstacles and bias, but politics was obviously not her forte.

Still running a successful law practice in 1957 at the age of seventy-three, and probably needing a respite from politics as well as her legal work, Felice spent a year traveling through Europe.

Maybe this was her grand tour, the one many girls of her generation enjoyed upon graduating from school. Felice had been too
young and too busy to go to traipsing around the world at that time.

On May 24, 1961, a warm spring day just ten days after her
seventy-seventh birthday, Felice Cohn died. The *Reno Evening Gazette*
ran a two-column spread listing the many firsts she accomplished
in her lifetime. A good number of her achievements in Nevada law
remain on the books today. She penetrated unopened doors seeking equal opportunities for Nevada's "delicate" gender, and dedicated herself to establishing organizations that promoted and
assisted women and children. Rising to heights and accomplish-
ments few of her sex had yet experienced, Felice Cohn traveled
through life with an independent spirit that remains the epitome
of today's Nevada woman.

BIBLIOGRAPHY

GENERAL BIBLIOGRAPHY

Davis, Sam P., ed. *The History of Nevada*. Las Vegas: Nevada Publications, 1984. Original publication Los Angeles: Elms Publishing Co., 1913.

DeQuille, Dan. *History of The Big Bonanza: An Authentic Account of the Discovery, History, and Working of the World Renowned Comstock Silver Lode of Nevada*. San Francisco: A. L. Bancroft & Co., 1876.

Elliott, Russell R. *History of Nevada, second edition revised*. Lincoln: University of Nebraska Press, 1987.

History of Nevada 1881 with Illustrations. Berkeley: Howell-North, 1958. Original publication, 1881.

James, Ronald M. *The Roar and the Silence: A History of Virginia City and the Comstock Lode*. Reno: University of Nevada Press, 1998.

James, Ronald M., and C. Elizabeth Raymond, eds. *Comstock Women: The Making of a Mining Community*. Reno: University of Nevada Press, 1998.

Lynn, Travis, narrator. *A Quiet Contribution: Women on the Comstock*. Nevada Experience Video No. 802. Carson City: Nevada State Library & Archives, 1998.

Mack, Effie Mona. *Nevada: A History of the State from the Earliest Times Through the Civil War*. Glendale, CA: The Arthur H. Clark Company, 1936.

Mathews, Mrs. M. M. *Ten Years in Nevada or Life on the Pacific Coast*. Lincoln: University of Nebraska Press, 1880.

Seagraves, Ann. *Women of the Sierra*. Hayden, ID: Wesanne Publications, 1990.

Watson, Anita Ernst. *Into Their Own: Nevada Women Emerging into Public Life*. A Halcyon Imprint of the Nevada Humanities Committee, 2000.

BIBLIOGRAPHY

Zanjani, Sally Springmeyer. *A Mine of Her Own: Women Prospectors in the American West, 1850–1950*. Lincoln: University of Nebraska Press, 1997.

ALISON EILLEY ORAM BOWERS

Addenbrooke, Alice B. *The Mistress of the Mansion*. Palo Alto: Pacific Books, 1950.

Earl, Phillip I. "A Woman of Fortune." *Nevada* 54, no. 2 (March–April 1994), 20–22.

Jeffries, Barbara J. *"Sandy" Bowers' Widow: The Biography of Allison "Eilley" Bowers*. Reno: Barringer Historical Books, 1993.

Mapes, Gloria Millicent, Maude Sawin Taylor, Ella Knowles Gottschalck, and Harriet Gaddis Spann. *Bowers Mansion*. Reno: Washoe County, 1952.

Payne, Swift. *Eilley Orrum: Queen of the Comstock*. Indianapolis: The Bobbs-Merrill Company, 1929.

Ratay, Myra Sauer. *Pioneers of the Ponderosa: How Washoe Valley Rescued the Comstock*. Sparks, NV: Western Printing and Publishing Company, 1973.

FERMINIA SARRAS

Hulse, James W. *The Silver State: Nevada's Heritage Reinterpreted*. Reno: University of Nevada Press, 1991.

Meadows, Lorena Edwards. *A Sagebrush Heritage: The Story of Ben Edwards and His Family*. San Jose: Harlan-Young Press, 1972.

Zanjani, Sally Springmeyer. *A Mine of Her Own: Women Prospectors in the American West, 1850–1950*. Lincoln: University of Nebraska Press, 1997.

BIBLIOGRAPHY

SARAH WINNEMUCCA HOPKINS

Butruille, Susan G. *Women's Voices from the Western Frontier.* Boise: Tamarack Books, Inc., 1995.

Canfield, Gae Whitney. *Sarah Winnemucca of the Northern Paiutes.* Norman: University of Oklahoma Press, 1983.

Dunlap, Patricia Riley. *Riding Astride: The Frontier Women's History.* Denver: Arden Press, Inc., 1995.

Hopkins, Sarah Winnemucca. *Life Among the Paiutes: Their Wrongs and Claims.* Edited by Mrs. Horace Mann. Boston: Cupples, Upham & Company, 1883.

McClure, Andrews S. "Sarah Winnemucca: [Post] Indian Princess and Voice of the Paiutes" (critical essay). Published by The Society for the Study of the Multi-Ethics Literature in the United States (MELUS), 24.2 (1999), 29–51. Accessed November 2, 2002, from www.findarticles .com/cf_0/m2278/2_24/59211506/print.jhtml.

Miller, Susan Cummins, ed. *A Sweet Separate Intimacy: Women Writers of the American Frontier, 1800–1922.* Salt Lake City: University of Utah Press, 2000.

Moynihan, Ruth B., Susan Armitage, and Christine Fisher Dichamp, eds. *So Much to Be Done: Women Settlers on the Mining and Ranching Frontier.* Lincoln: University of Nebraska Press, 1990.

Schlissel, Lilliam, and Catherine Lavender, eds. *The Western Women's Reader: The Remarkable Writings of Women Who Shaped the American West, Spanning 300 Years.* New York: Harper Perennial, 2000.

Stewart, Patricia. "Sarah Winnemucca." *Nevada Historical Society Quarterly* 14, no. 4 (winter 1971), 23–38.

Zanjani, Sally Springmeyer. *Sarah Winnemucca.* Lincoln: University of Nebraska Press, 2001.

BIBLIOGRAPHY

DAT SO LA LEE

Cohodas, Marvin. "Dat so la lee and the Degikup." *Halcyon, A Journal of the Humanities* (1982), 119–140.

———. "Louisa Keyser and the Cohns: Mythmaking and Basket Making in the American West." *The Early Years of Native American Art History.* Janet Catherine Berlo, ed. Seattle: University of Washington Press, 1992, 88–133.

Hickson, Jane Green. *Dat So La Lee: Queen of the Washo Basketmakers.* Carson City: Nevada State Museum Popular Series, December 1967.

Ross, Christopher. "Dat So La Lee and the Myth Weavers." *Nevada Magazine* (September–October 1989).

HELEN JANE STEWART

Seagraves, Anne. *High-Spirited Women of the West.* Lakeport, CA: Wesanne Publications, 1992.

Porter, Carrie Miller Townley. Personal interview, April 29, 2003. Personal correspondence, various dates.

Townley, Carrie Miller. "Helen J. Stewart: First Lady of Las Vegas." Part 1. *Nevada Historical Society Quarterly* 16, no. 4 (winter 1973), 215–244.

———. "Helen J. Stewart: First Lady of Las Vegas." Part 2. *Nevada Historical Society Quarterly* 17, no. 1 (spring 1974), 3–32.

IDAH MEACHAM STROBRIDGE

Amaral, Anthony. "Idah Mecham Strobridge: First Woman of Nevada Letters." *Nevada Historical Society Quarterly* 9 (fall 1967), 5–12.

Laxalt, Robert. *Nevada: A Bicentennial History.* Reno: University of Nevada Press, 1977.

BIBLIOGRAPHY

Nugent, Walter. *Into the West: The Story of Its People.* New York: Vintage Books, 2001.

Roland, Ann. "Idah Meacham Strobridge: The Second Mary Austin?" (essay). *Weber Studies Literary Journal,* Weber State University College of Arts and Humanities, Ogden, Utah, 11.1 (spring–summer 1994).

"Splendid Ranch for Sale." Advertisement for sale of Strobridge ranch. *Land of Sunshine,* November 1900.

Strobridge, Idah Meacham. *Sagebrush Trilogy: Idah Meacham Strobridge and Her Works.* Introduction by Richard Dwyer and Richard E. Longenfelter. Reno: University of Nevada Press, 1990.

ELIZA COOK

Abram, Ruth J., ed. *"Send Us a Lady Physician": Women Doctors in America, 1835–1920.* New York: W. W. Norton & Company, 1985.

Cook, Eliza. "Outline of My Life." Original document found beside Dr. Cook at the time of her death, 1947.

Jones, Cherry. Personal correspondence. December 2003–January 2004.

Luchetti, Cathy. *Medicine Women: The Story of Early-American Women Doctors.* New York: Crown Publishers, 1998.

Sohn, Anton P. *The Healers of 19th-Century Nevada.* Reno: Greasewood Press, 1997.

DAUGHTERS OF CHARITY

Beaupre, Carolyn, archivist, St. Mary's of the Mountains Church. Personal interview, April 29, 2003.

Butler, Anne M., Michael E. Engh, SJ, and Thomas W. Spalding, CFX, eds. *The Frontiers and Catholic Identities.* Maryknoll, NY: Orbis Books, 1999.

BIBLIOGRAPHY

Cooley, Cora. Correspondence addressed to St. Mary's in the Mountains Church, Virginia City, NV, August 20, 1947.

Daughters of Charity, Seaton Provincialate. *Our Treasured Past: Daughters of Charity of St. Vincent de Paul.* Los Altos, CA: Daughters of Charity, 2002.

Gainey, Sister Margaret Ann. Daughters of Charity, Seton Provincialate, Los Altos Hills, CA. Telephone interview, July 28, 2003.

Gorman, Most Reverend Thomas K., compiler. *Seventy-Five Years of Catholic Life in Nevada.* Reno: The Journal Press, 1935.

Hedrick, Georgia. "The Great White Birds That Prayed." *Nevada Woman* 3, no. 4 (January–February 1998), 52–58.

———. Telephone interview, August 1, 2003. Personal correspondence, various dates.

Oberding, Janice. *Haunted Nevada.* Accessed July 28, 2003, from www.u publish.com/books/oberding.htm. Universal Publishers, 2001.

"Remarks on Sister Alice McGrath, who died April 18th, 1913, at Mount St. Joseph's Infant Asylum, San Francisco, California, 88 years of age, 69 of vocation." *Lives of Our Deceased Sisters, 1913.* Privately bound edition.

Sister Frederica McGrath. Obituary. *San Francisco Monitor* 54, no. 49 (April 26, 1913), 1, 8.

Weatherly, Bonnie, archivist, Daughters of Charity, St. Joseph Provincial House, Emmitsburg, MD. Personal correspondence, August 27, 28, 2003.

JOSEPHINE REED PEARL

Murbarger, Nell. *Sovereigns of the Sage.* Tucson: Treasure Chest Publishing, 1958.

Pyle, Ernie. *Home Country.* New York: William Sloane Associates, Inc., 1947.

BIBLIOGRAPHY

Read, Effie Oxborrow. *White Pine Lang Syne: A True History of White Pine Country.* Denver: Big Mountain Press, 1965.

Schulmerich, Alma. *Josie Pearl.* Salt Lake City: Deseret Book Company, 1963.

ANNE HENRIETTA MARTIN

Anderson, Kathryn. "Anne Martin and the Dream of Political Equality for Women." *Journal of the West* (April 1988), 28–34.

Basso, Dave. *Anne Martin: Pioneer Nevada Feminist: Selected Writings.* Sparks, NV: Falcon Hill Press, 1986.

Ford, Jean, and James W. Hulse. "The First Battle for Woman Suffrage in Nevada: 1869–1871—Correcting and Expanding the Record." *Nevada Historical Society Quarterly* 38, no. 3 (fall 1995), 174–188.

Howard, Anne Bail. *The Long Campaign: A Biography of Anne Martin.* Reno: University of Nevada Press, 1985.

Martin, Anne. "These United States—VII; Nevada: Beautiful Desert of Buried Hopes." *The Nation* (July 26, 1922), 89–92.

Shepperson, Wilbur S. *Mirage-Land: Images of Nevada.* Reno: University of Nevada Press, 1992.

Smith, Ann Warren. *Anne Martin and a History of Woman Suffrage in Nevada, 1869–1914.* A dissertation submitted in partial fulfillment of the requirements for the degree of Doctor of Philosophy in History. Reno: University of Nevada, 1975.

Wilson, B. M. "The Story of the Nevada Equal Suffrage Campaign: Memoirs of Anne Martin." Edited and with an introduction by Anne E. Hutcheson. *University of Nevada Bulletin* 42, no. 7 (August 1948), 3–19.

BIBLIOGRAPHY

AH CUM KEE

Au, Beth Amity. *Home Means Nevada: The Chinese in Winnemucca, Nevada, 1870–1950: A Narrative History.* Thesis. Los Angeles: University of California, 1993.

Baldwin, Shirlaine, granddaughter of Ah Cum Kee. Telephone interview, August 24, 2003. Personal correspondence, various dates.

BeDunnah, Gary P. *A History of the Chinese in Nevada: 1855–1904.* Thesis. Reno: University of Nevada, 1966.

Chan, Loren B. "The Chinese in Nevada: An Historical Survey, 1856–1970." *Nevada Historical Society Quarterly* 25, no. 4 (winter 1982), 266–315.

Chung, Sue Fawn. "The Chinese Experience in Nevada: Success Despite Discrimination." *Nevada Public Affairs Review* 2 (1987), 43–51.

Lindenmeyer, Kriste, ed. *Ordinary Women, Extraordinary Lives: Women in American History.* Wilmington, DE: Scholarly Resources Inc., 2000.

Luchetti, Cathy, and Carol Olwell. *Women of the West.* New York: Orion Books, 1982.

Magnaghi, Russell M. "Virginia City's Chinese Community, 1860–1880." *Nevada Historical Society Quarterly* 24, no. 2 (summer 1981), 130–157.

Sigerman, Harriet. *Land of Many Hands: Women in the American West.* New York: Oxford University Press, 1997.

MAUDE FRAZIER

Cummings, Nancy R., and Dorothy Ritenour, compilers and writers. *County School Legacy: Humanities on the Frontier: Report from Southern Nevada,* 1981.

Davies, Richard O., ed. *The Maverick Spirit: Building the New Nevada.* Reno: University of Nevada Press, 1999.

BIBLIOGRAPHY

Frazier, Maude. *Autobiography/Maude Frazier*. Las Vegas: University of Nevada, Las Vegas Special Collections, 1960.

Glass, Mary Ellen. *Maude Frazier*. Prepared for Notable American Women. Reno: University of Nevada, 1978.

Hulse, James W. *The Maverick Spirit: Building the New Nevada*. Reno: University of Nevada Press, 1999.

FELICE COHN

Binheim, Max, ed. *Women of the West: A Series of Biographical Sketches of Living Eminent Women in the Eleven Western Sates of the United States of America*. Los Angeles: Publishers Press, 1928.

"Felice Cohn—A Woman of Action." *Nevada State Journal*, May 2, 1932.

Rocha, Guy. *Stepping Up to the Bar: Female Attorneys in Nevada*. Nevada Library and Archives Myth 72. Accessed August 7, 2002, from http://dmla.clan.lib.nv.us/docs/nsla/archives/myth/myth72.htm. Originally published in *Sierra Sage*, Carson City/Carson Valley, NV, January 2002.

INDEX

INDEX

BOUT THE AUTHOR

When Jan Cleere wrote *Stinky the Easter Skunk* and *The Mischievous Monkey* at the age of eleven, she was well on her way to becoming a writer even though *Humpty Dumpty Magazine* did not share her enthusiasm for her first submissions. After running a family business and rearing three children, she returned to school, receiving her degree in American Studies from Arizona State University West. She writes extensively for regional publications, covering topics ranging from travel to capturing elusive pack rats, but her first love is writing the histories of pioneering women whose stories lay dormant for years beneath the desert asphalt. Jan lives with her husband in Oro Valley, Arizona, where she often discovers coyotes, javelina, bobcats, and an occasional mountain lion devouring her desert blooms.

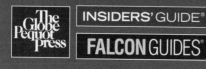